The Mysterious British Isles: A Collection of Mysteries, Legends, and Unexplained Phenomena across Britain and Ireland

By Sean McLachlan and Charles River Editors

Anne Burgess' picture of a Pictish Stone

About Charles River Editors

Charles River Editors is a boutique digital publishing company, specializing in bringing history back to life with educational and engaging books on a wide range of topics. Keep up to date with our new and free offerings with this 5 second sign up on our weekly mailing list, and visit Our Kindle Author Page to see other recently published Kindle titles.

We make these books for you and always want to know our readers' opinions, so we encourage you to leave reviews and look forward to publishing new and exciting titles each week.

About the Author

Sean McLachlan spent many years working as an archaeologist in Europe, the Middle East, and the United States. Now a full-time writer, he's the author of many history books and novels, including *A Fine Likeness*, a Civil War novel with a touch of the paranormal. Feel free to visit him on his Amazon page and blog.

Introduction

An Anglo-Saxon belt buckle depicting the god Woden (Odin)

Mysterious Great Britain

"The Anglo-Saxon charms… are of outstanding importance because they provide more than vague references of exceptional and short texts. They cannot be said to reveal everything, for there are numerous points in which they lamentably fail us, but they are numerous enough and, taken as a body, complete enough to give more than a tantalising hint of a strange world. The veil of mystification enveloping magic appears to be thin and transparent here." - G. Storms, *Anglo-Saxon Magic* (1948)

Great Britain is an ancient land steeped in history and tradition, filled with prehistoric ruins, majestic castles, and a countryside sculpted from millennia of human habitation.. Its rolling countryside is dotted with prehistoric burial mounds and stone circles. Brooding castles hold tales of bloodshed and honor. Medieval churches have elaborate stained glass windows and gruesome carvings, reflecting a mixture of hope and darkness. Every hamlet and village has tales that go back centuries, and folk festivals with roots in pagan times.

Not everything in Great Britain is as it appears, however. Some say this is a land haunted by spirits, a place of strange disappearances and unexplained phenomena. For centuries, people have told tales of ghosts stalking its historic buildings, strange creatures lurking in its primeval forests, and unexplained paths linking its ancient sites. There is no shortage when it comes to the strange stories the region has to offer, and the legends and lore have compelled many to dig a little deeper and even explore this wonderful land for themselves.

Ireland also has a rich folklore. Everyone knows about the fairy folk and leprechauns and many have heard of the fearsome banshee, and there are also the usual ghost stories found in every old land. The stranger side of the Emerald Isle goes much deeper than that, however, with tales of phantom armies marching through the sky, sea monsters swimming in the waters around the island, and stories of strange powers and dark magic.

Indeed, these tales are not consigned to the past; many unexplained occurrences continue to happen, even today. Here is a sampling of some of Ireland's odder aspects Ireland. Hopefully, it will inspire readers to learn more about Ireland's mysterious past and unusual present, and perhaps get readers to visit Ireland themselves.

The Mysterious British Isles: A Collection of Mysteries, Legends, and Unexplained Phenomena across Britain and Ireland offers a sampling of the many strange stories and unexplained phenomena that make Britain and Ireland such intriguing places. Along with pictures of important people, places, and events, you will learn about the weird legends and mysteries of the British Isles like never before.

The Mysterious British Isles: A Collection of Mysteries, Legends, and Unexplained Phenomena across Britain and Ireland

About Charles River Editors

About the Author

Introduction

    Traces of Ancient London

    Rotten Scoundrels

    Odd Old Professions

    Magicians and Witches

    Strange English Creatures

    Fatbergs

    Ley Lines

    Holy Wells

    Charms and Spells

    Hummadruz

    English Ghosts

    Spring-heeled Jack

    The Devil's Footprints

    Crop Circles

    Strange Scottish Creatures

    The Horrible History of Sawney Beane

    Scottish Ghosts and Spirits

    Scottish Mysteries

    An Ancient Irish Mystery

    Strange Irish Creatures of the Deep

    Irish Ghosts, Banshees, and Phantom Ships

    Apparitions of the Blessed Virgin Mary

    Fairy Folk

    Witches, Cunning Folk, and other Magical People

    Watching the Skies

    The Weird and Unexplainable

    Online Resources

    Further Reading

Free Books by Charles River Editors

Discounted Books by Charles River Editors

Traces of Ancient London

For most of the past 1,000 years, London has been the most dominant city in the world, ruling over so much land that it was said the Sun never set on the British Empire. With the possible exception of Rome, no city has ever been more important or influential than London in human history. Thus, it was only fitting that it was the Romans who established London as a prominent city.

Londinium was initially little more than a small military outpost near the northern boundary of the Roman province of Britannia, but its access to the River Thames and the North Sea made it a valuable location for a port. During the middle of the first century A.D., the Romans conducted another invasion of the British Isles, after which Londinium began to grow rapidly. As the Romans stationed legions there to defend against the Britons, Londinium became a thriving international port, allowing trade with Rome and other cities across the empire.

By the 2nd century CE, Londinium was a large Roman city, with tens of thousands of inhabitants using villas, palaces, a forum, temples, and baths. The Roman governor ruled from the city in a basilica that served as the seat of government. What was once a 30 acre outpost now spanned 300 acres and was home to nearly 15,000 people, including Roman soldiers, officials and foreign merchants. The Romans also built heavy defenses for the city, constructing several forts and the massive London Wall, parts of which are still scattered across the city today.

As a result, London is an amalgamation of the ancient, the old, and the new. Churches are built atop pagan temples, subway tunnels cut through medieval burial grounds, and skyscrapers cast shadows over Tudor homes. Everywhere one looks, the past peeks out from cracks in the modern façade.

Researchers have found convincing evidence that some of the city's most important political and religious sites are actually situated on old pagan religious spots. This was common practice in the days of early Christianity as a way to symbolically defeat the old ways. There's an old London legend that St. Paul's was built on an old Roman temple to Diana, goddess of the hunt, atop Ludgate Hill. The Romans often just renamed deities taken from the Greek pantheon, and Diana's Greek equivalent was Artemis.

St. Paul was famous for suppressing the worship of Artemis at Ephesus, which may explain why the church was dedicated to that particular saint. Significantly, during the Middle Ages, the surrounding buildings were called the *Camera Dianae*. During the reign of Edward I (1274-1307), a huge number of ox heads were found in the churchyard, believed to have been used as sacrifices at the old temple.

St. Paul's Cathedral

Traces of the cult did not disappear entirely. Before the Reformation got rid of many popular festivals, St. Paul's was the site of an annual "Blowing of the Stag," a ceremony in which the head of a stag was carried on the end of a spear into the church and laid upon the altar. Huntsmen would go around the woods surrounding the city, blowing horns in the four cardinal directions.

To the west of St. Paul's stands London's other major religious center, Westminster Abbey. It almost goes without saying that Westminster Abbey is one of the foremost sites in Europe when it comes to being steeped in history. Dating back to the reign of William the Conqueror and the Norman conquest, Westminster Abbey has traditionally been the site of royal coronations, royal weddings, and royal burials, and anyone who enters can instantly feel that they are walking in the footsteps of some of the most influential figures in history, from Henry III to Queen Elizabeth I.

Of course, Westminster Abbey is also far more than a place for royalty. As the English became to more intimately associate the site with their history and culture, luminaries from all walks of life have also been interred there, from Charles Darwin and Isaac Newton to Rudyard Kipling and Charles Dickens. Along with effigies, plaques, and various other monuments, walking through Westminster Abbey offers its own sort of crash course on England over the centuries.

While Westminster Abbey has been an important site for nearly 1,000 years, it is perhaps unsurprising that it has had a volatile history, a byproduct of England's own tumultuous past. As a religious site first and foremost, the Abbey was at the forefront of the religious unrest that occasionally swept the British Isles, whether it was Henry VIII's formation of the Church of England or his devoutly Catholic daughter earning the sobriquet Bloody Mary. As a result of it all, the Abbey has served different religious purposes over the course of time as well.

In medieval times, Westminster Abbey stood on the Isle of Thorney, formed by a confluence of the Tyburn and the Thames. Legend has it that this was the site of a Roman temple of Apollo. He was the sun god and his sister Artemis was the moon goddess. This temple was said to have been destroyed by an earthquake and later replaced with an Anglo-Saxon temple to Thor.

The site was made Christian in 610 CE by Sæberht, King of the East Saxons, who had converted to Christianity and proved his loyalty to the new faith by erecting the first church on the spot. It may indeed have been the first church in London, although there are other claimants to that honor and no one knows for sure.

The church was to be dedicated to St. Peter, and legend has it that the night before the consecration, St. Peter himself descended from heaven to sanctify the church. He landed at Lambeth, on the south side of the river. Disguising himself as an ordinary mortal, he asked a fisherman named Edric to ferry him across. Edric complied and got the surprise of his life. As

Peter entered the church, the interior shone with a brilliant light. Angelic voices rose up in song and prayer. St. Peter then emerged and asked Edric to take him to Mellitus, the Archbishop of London and the man who had converted King Sæberht. When they got there, Peter informed the archbishop of his true identity and that the church had already been consecrated. His holy work finished, the saint ascended back up to heaven.

Another ancient holdover is the oddly named street Houndsditch, which runs through the City of London, the financial heart of the city that corresponds to the old Roman Londinium. Traces of the Roman city wall along Noble St. can still be spotted from the windows of the Museum of London, and nearby a Roman temple of Mithras was uncovered in 1954 and preserved for visitors.

Houndsditch, however, has a stranger, more evocative story. Much of the street passes along the outside of the old Roman wall and served as a dumping ground for all sorts of refuse. An archaeological excavation underneath part of the road in 1989 found canine skeletons dating from the Roman period. Although the ditch was filled in the 16th century and turned into a street, the memory of old Londinium's dumping ground is still preserved in the name.

A statue of Trajan in front of the ruins of a Roman wall in London

Walking down Houndsditch, visitors will notice that the modern buildings often leave part of their plots unused. Visiting Pitfield Street in Hoxton, Islington Green on Upper Street, and several other spots around the city, visitors will notice the same thing. With every square meter of real estate commanding high prices, this might seem an odd thing to do, but this too is an echo of the past. These bits of empty lands in the crowded city are old plague pits, mass graves that were used to dispose of hundreds of infected corpses during the many times the plague has swept through London.

England was first visited by the plague during the great European epidemic of 1348. It hit London in the summer of that year as the bubonic plague and turned into the more dangerous pneumonic plague by autumn. It killed thousands in London and an estimated 15 percent of England's total population. London may have lost up to half its population. One chronicler recorded that "the plague raged to such a degree that the living were scarce able to bury the dead." At a mass grave in Smithfield, more than 200 bodies a day were dumped into a big pit and hastily covered over with earth. The unfortunate victims were laid out in stacks five deep. The Smithfield pit was only one of dozens scattered throughout the city.

Plague spread so quickly because London, like other medieval cities, was a cesspool of filth. Residents lived cheek by jowl in crowded tenements. People tossed their human waste out the window or down stinking, overfilled outhouses. Refuse ran down the roads or congealed in putrid pools open to the air. Rats infested everything and the Thames, where people got their drinking water, ran ripe with human waste, dead animals, and rotting food. King Edward III realized that these horrible conditions only made the plague worse and ordered the city council to clean up the streets. The council replied that they would like to, but all their street cleaners had all succumbed to the plague. At Westminster Abbey, visitors to the southern cloister can see a black slab that covers the body of the Abbot of Westminster and 27 of his monks, all victims of the terrible pestilence.

A posthumous portrait of Edward III

The plague disappeared by 1350, but it came back again in 1361-64, 1368, 1371, 1373-75, 1390, and 1405. There were several recurrences after that, the worst being from 1665 to 1666. This horrible epidemic killed off an estimated 100,000 people, a quarter of the population, in just 18 months. Plague did not finally disappear from England until after 1750.

Plague pits are scattered throughout the city, remembered in local folklore and planning regulations. In some parts, it is still forbidden to build upon them. A grassy area on the appropriately named Pitfield Street in Hoxton has a sign warning people to "Keep off the Grass." Perhaps the local council is afraid that the bodies below still might carry contagion?

One of the city's oldest monuments is also the easiest to miss. Tucked behind a metal grill on the outer wall of 111 Cannon Street is an unassuming lump of stone. The stone measures 21 inches by 17 inches by 12 inches and is oolitic limestone, a type of stone not found in the Thames River Valley. It is called the London Stone and has been a part of London's history since the beginning, gathering a large amount of folklore around it. It first appears in written record around the end of the 11th century, being called the London Stone and only given passing reference without explanation, meaning the medieval writers assumed the reader would know what it was.

It's too bad these early chroniclers didn't explain further, because just what purpose the London Stone originally served has been a matter of debate ever since. Some writers think that it was an old Roman *milliarium*, a measuring stone used as a zero point from which to make measurements across the province of Britannia. Cannon Street is, indeed, a Roman road, set in the heart of the old Roman Londinium.

Others think that it is the last remains of a Neolithic stone circle or even a mark stone for the famous ley lines, lines of religious power that ran through the ancient landscape. A more fanciful theory hold that Brutus of Troy fled his ruined city after the Trojan War and settled in Britain, founding London as the New Troy. This theory was much in vogue in the days of the Enlightenment, when the educated class admired the classics, but there is no evidence it's true.

The London Stone

Whatever the stone originally was, it captured the imagination of the city. The city's first mayor, Henry Fitz-Ailwin, lived next to the stone in the 12th century. In fact, he often signed his name "Henry Fitz-Ailwin of Londonestone." At that time it was much bigger, a large rectangular monolith that sat in the middle of the road. Carts and pedestrians had to move around it. Despite this annoyance, no one thought to move it. At the Museum of London, one can study the first detailed map of the city, the so-called "Copperplate" map of 1559. There on Candlewick Street, the former name for Cannon Street, the stone is shown as a rectangular block in the middle of the road right opposite the door to St. Swithin's church.

In 1450, a rebel from Kent named Jack Cade took the city from the corrupt and abusive King Henry VI and struck his sword against the stone to declare himself "Lord of London" in a ceremony that some sources say had become tradition by this time. Despite his claim to legitimacy, His Lordship didn't last long and was hunted down and killed by the High Sheriff of Kent that same year.

Henry VI

The stone remained a noted landmark, and according to some sources, it was used as a meeting place for debtors to pay off their loans, the deal being sealed by both parties placing their hands on the stone. The London Stone caught the imagination of no less a figure than the great mystic poet William Blake, who wrote in his 1804 poem *Jerusalem*:

"And the Druids' golden Knife Rioted in human gore,

In Offerings of Human Life...

They groan'd aloud on London Stone,

They groan'd aloud on Tyburn's Brook."

Blake saw it as a bloody pagan altar and compared it with Tyburn, the notorious spot of execution.

Blake

The London Stone was damaged in the Great Fire of 1666 but remained in the middle of the road until increased traffic caused it to be moved to a new location beside the entrance to St. Swithin's church in 1742. It was later moved inside and eventually ended up in its present condition in 1962. It's not known when it was reduced to such a small size. Now it lies neglected, with the rushing crowds rarely even noticing its existence.

Rotten Scoundrels

London is a place where many have gone to find their fortune. Most never do. It can be a cruel city, one that can grind a person down into poverty and degradation. Before the 20th century, it was not uncommon for some Londoners to starve to death. Because of extreme want, or simple greed, more than a few city residents turned to crime. They, too, are part of London's colorful history.

The city has produced many notorious criminals, but none have gained so much fame for so little success as Colonel Thomas Blood. He came from a wealthy family in Ireland who lost their fortune in the 1662 Act of Settlement, which after the Restoration of the monarchy following the English Civil War took back lands granted under Oliver Cromwell's reign. Blood never forgot the ruin of his family's fortune and swore revenge. After a failed attack on the Castle of Dublin, he and his men sailed to London to assassinate the Duke of Ormond, one of the main royalists who had convinced King Charles II to pass the act.

Blood

On December 6, 1670, he waylaid the Duke's retinue on St. James Street. He and his men charged out of the surrounding crowd, swords in hand, and quickly overpowered the Duke's guards. His strongest man hauled the Duke onto his horse and tied their belts together so the Duke couldn't escape. The kidnappers then headed for the public gallows at Tyburn, near where Marble Arch stands today, so they could humiliate the Duke by hanging him like a common criminal. Blood was so eager for his revenge that he rushed ahead to tie the noose so all would be ready when his prisoner arrived.

The Duke must have sensed what his fate would be because he threw himself off the horse, taking his guard with him. Both landed in the mud just as reinforcements from the Duke's mansion ran up. After a short swordfight, all the conspirators were captured or driven off.

Colonel Blood escaped when he discovered the Duke had been rescued, and he would be heard from again, this time with a greater goal in mind. Early the following year, Colonel Blood appeared at the Tower of London dressed as a clergyman and accompanied by a woman he claimed was his wife. They asked Talbot Edwards, the aged custodian of the Crown Jewels, to be shown the priceless crown and scepter in the Jewel Tower. While today the jewels are protected by bulletproof glass and CCTV, back then they were protected only by an iron grating inside a castle manned by soldiers. Blood could have attempted a robbery then and there, but he had a more refined plan; instead, his female companion acted ill and was taken to the quarters of the Edwards family, where the lady of the house took care of her. After the woman said she felt better, the "couple" left.

Blood returned a few days later bringing presents to thank the family for their kindness to his wife. He soon insinuated himself into their friendship and became a regular visitor inside the Tower. Finally, he broached the offer of marrying his nephew to the Warden's daughter. He regaled them with tales of his nephew's fine lands and wealth. They agreed to introduce the two on May 9, 1671, and Blood managed to get permission to bring some friends to see the jewels.

Having gained consent to bring an unusually large number of people into the Tower, Blood prepared to strike. Blood and three others arrived at an early hour, each with a pair of pistols and a dagger hidden under their cloaks and rapiers hidden in their walking sticks. While the hopeful bride primped in front of a mirror upstairs, Blood and two others went to see the jewels while the fourth man, playing the nephew, stayed at the front door supposedly waiting for the woman. His real job was to keep an eye on the guards manning the walls and gates. When Edwards led the three men into the Jewel House, Blood closed the door behind them and the others stuffed a gag into the keeper's mouth, put a bag over his head, and told him to keep quiet, or they'd kill him.

Edwards may have been a frail old man, but he knew his duty and sent up a huge racket, hoping his family upstairs would hear. The robbers knocked him down with a wooden mallet they'd brought to flatten the crown and stabbed him, and when he continued to make noise, they hit him over the head again until he fell unconscious. The robbers then pried open the metal grille that protected the jewels and pulled out the loot. Blood hid the crown under his cloak while another thief put the orb in his breeches. A third grabbed the scepter.

Just then, Edwards' son happened to show up with a friend. Blood and his crew panicked and fled, just as the older Edwards pulled the gag off and shouted, "Treason! Murder!" His daughter ran out into the courtyard to give the alarm. The Warder blocked the exit, but Blood shot him and the conspirators rushed out of the Tower, a crowd of guards at their heels.

It wasn't long before they ran him to ground, with Blood crying out in despair, "It was a gallant attempt, however unsuccessful, for it was for a crown!" The guards soon hunted down the rest of the gang and retrieved all the crown jewels.

Now came the strangest part of this tale. When dragged before King Charles II, Blood launched into an eloquent speech about how his family had been wronged and that he had once planned to shoot Charles while the king was swimming in the Thames. When he spied the king in all his regal splendor, he claimed that "his heart was checked by an awe of Majesty."

Charles II

This suited the king's vanity, and he pardoned the conspirators, even giving Blood some land in Ireland. In fact, he rewarded Blood for attempting to steal the jewels more than he awarded Edwards and his son for stopping him. Blood became a member of the court until he was put in jail for libeling his patron, the Duke of Buckingham. He fell ill in prison and died on August 24, 1680. In *History of Insipids*, John Wilmot, 2nd Earl of Rochester, colorfully described the change in Blood's fortunes and makes light of it:

"Blood, that wears treason in his face,

Villain complete in parson's gown,

How much he is at court in grace

For stealing Ormond and the crown!

Since loyalty does no man good,

Let's steal the King, and outdo Blood!"

Wilmot

William Henry Ireland was a less adventurous, more cerebral crook. When later asked about his misdeeds, he claimed all he wanted to do was make his father happy. Samuel Ireland was a Shakespeare fanatic, dragging his son to every spot the Bard had lived or worked while pontificating about the greatness of the famous playwright, so William decided to have a bit of harmless fun. In 1793, the 18 year old forged a mortgage deed between Shakespeare and his landlord and gave it to his father as a gift, claiming he bought it from a dealer in rare books. Samuel Ireland was ecstatic, so William wrote up some more documents, including a love letter from Shakespeare to his future wife Anne Hathaway that had a lock of Shakespeare's hair attached.

Ireland

Enjoying a closeness with his father he had never before experienced, William got bolder and penned an entire play titled "Vortigern and Rowena." His forgery was well crafted; he used period paper that he ripped out the flyleafs of old books and got a bookbinder to make up some ink in the fashion of the 16th century.

Eventually, the unusual gifts to his father got out of hand. The Shakespeare lover bragged about his son's discoveries, and their house was soon besieged by curiosity seekers. Most self-proclaimed experts stated the documents appeared genuine, and two even got down on their knees to pay homage to the supposedly undiscovered play, but there were also skeptics right from the beginning. A new Shakespeare play simply had to be performed on stage, and Richard Sheridan of the Drury Lane Theatre offered William Ireland £300 plus royalties to perform it. While Sheridan harbored doubts as to the play's authenticity, he had no doubts that it would sell tickets.

And sell it did. On opening night a huge crowd packed the theatre, and the spectacle of the play's supporters and detractors screaming at one another proved as entertaining as the play itself. Ireland turned out to be a talented playwright, and while he couldn't match Shakespeare's magic with words, he did create a good bit of theatre, both onstage and off. Opening night was almost spoiled by actor John Kemble, who played the lead character as poorly as he could in order to undermine the performance. When he got to the line "and when this solemn mockery is o'er," he repeated it with emphasis and the audience howled in derision.

Kemble

The play didn't run the following night. By this time, one of the major Shakespeare authorities had published an extensive analysis of Ireland's documents that proved beyond doubt they were forgeries. This got extensive coverage in the press, and William had to go into hiding, though he eventually wrote a confession that became a bestseller in its own right. After a while, the whole affair died down, and the only real victims were the Ireland's. The father was heartbroken by the deceit, and the son found his literary aspirations blocked by his reputation as a forger. He did, however, achieve lasting fame as one of Shakespeare's most successful imitators.

Far less savory than these two characters were the resurrection men, a product of an unsavory time. The early days of medicine were not a good time to fall ill, as doctors bled patients, put leeches on them, and forced them to swallow noxious brews in the hope they would somehow get better. Any success was generally due to the luck or strength of the patient, not the skill of the doctor, though few understood that. Indeed, a visit to the Old Operating Theatre is Southwark, which displays medical equipment from those early years, will cure anyone of their complaints about modern medicine.

Doctors were not entirely to blame for this grim state of affairs. Until the mid-19th century, dissection of cadavers was a crime. Surgeons could only use bodies of criminals sentenced to death and dissection, considered such a horrible punishment that the courts reserved it only for the worst murderers. In their quest for knowledge, doctors took to buying the corpses of the recently dead from "resurrection men," who dug up fresh graves to supply corpses for study.

One case occurred in Bloomsbury on the evening of October 9, 1777. A certain Mr. Eustanston and some friends were passing by the burial ground of St. George the Martyr when they came across Robert Williams, assistant gravedigger for the church, lugging a large sack over his shoulder and accompanied by another man. Both were heading for the Foundling Hospital.

This must have aroused Eustanston's suspicions because he stopped them and demanded to know what was in the bag. Williams, not being the sharpest shovel in the graveyard, claimed he didn't know and pleaded to be let go, saying he was "a poor man just come from harvest." Eustanston grabbed the sack and to his horror discovered the body of a woman trussed up like a hog. Eustanston and his friends were so stunned that Williams' companion got away, but they did manage to grab the gravedigger.

The next day the police went to the graveyard and interviewed John Holmes, the head gravedigger, who he said he didn't know Williams. Not fooled by this obvious lie, they searched the burial ground and found an upturned plot with an empty coffin just a few inches below the ground. As they were doing this, they spotted Holmes hiding bits of shroud in his pocket. They put him under arrest.

The body was identified as a woman who had died earlier that month. In court, the attorney for the defense made the argument that stealing a dead body was not, in fact, illegal - only selling it to a surgeon was. That argument didn't wash, however, and both gravediggers got six months in prison.

A more successful resurrection duo was John Bishop and Thomas Williams, executed in 1831 for murder. Not content with simply digging up the dead—Bishop claimed to have exhumed more than 500 corpses over a 12 year period—they lured homeless women and children into their family cottage and, while their wives and children slept, drugged them with laudanum and drowned them in the well. They were caught when their regular customers, being physicians, noticed the bodies appeared too fresh to have been buried and dug up. Their subsequent trial and execution were the sensation of the year.

Bishop, Williams, and James May

This and other prominent trials of resurrection men led to the Anatomy Act of 1832, allowing all unclaimed bodies from prisons and workhouses to be used for examination. Given that London was a poor and violent place, these two institutions more than met the demands of medical science, and the days of the resurrection men were over.

When looking for victims, some criminals aimed higher than moldering corpses; in fact, they aimed for the highest man in the land. While King George III (reigned 1761-1820) has gone down in American history as the mad monarch who overtaxed the colonies and tried to suppress the American War of Independence, it is often forgotten that he wasn't particularly popular at home either. Nevertheless, there were only two attempts on his life during his 59-year reign, both by persons judged to be insane.

George III

The first occurred on August 2, 1786, as the king stepped out of his post-chariot at the garden entrance to James Palace. A commonly dressed woman waiting there for him handed him a paper. This was a normal occurrence, as people gave petitions to the king all the time, and he graciously took it and bowed to the woman. That bow saved his life because it took him out of the way of a knife thrust at his chest. His guards and servants immediately tackled her, while George, examining a slight tear in his waistcoat, said, "I have received no injury; do not hurt the woman, the poor creature appears insane." The woman turned out to be Margaret Nicholson. Judges found her insane and committed her to Bethlehem Hospital, popularly known as "Bedlam," where she lived to be 99 years old.

A more serious attack occurred on May 15, 1800, when the royal family attended a play at the Drury Lane Theatre. Just as George stepped into the box, a man in one of the front rows stood up and discharged a pistol at him. For a moment the theatre fell silent, and then the crowd raised the cry, "Seize the villain! Shut the doors!" A gentleman standing next to the would-be assassin grabbed him and dragged him into the orchestra, where he was disarmed and hustled backstage.

One of the actors dramatically held the pistol aloft for all to see while the king stood in his box assuring everyone he was safe.

Mr. Sheridan, the theatre's owner, showed his famous sense of the dramatic by quickly penning an extra verse to "God Save the King," and had his band strike up the tune as he sang out the new lines,

> "From every latent foe,
>
> From the assassin's blow,
>
> O'er him Thine arm extend,
>
> From every ill defend,
>
> Our Father, King, and Friend,
>
> God save the King!"

This brought the house down, and the play went on as scheduled. Ironically, the king promptly fell asleep anyway.

The gunman was James Hadfield, a former dragoon who had been wounded fighting the French in Flanders. He claimed he had become "tired of life" and had chosen a rather unorthodox way to die. The judges, however, declared him insane and committed him to the lunatic asylum of Bedlam, now the Imperial War Museum, where he spent the remaining 41 years of his life. There he kept cats and birds and wrote moving elegies to them when they died. He occasionally received visitors, and the general impression was that he was not out of his mind but severely melancholic. It is not recorded whether he ever met his fellow inmate and failed assassin Margaret Nicholson, but since men and women were strictly segregated, it is unlikely.

A depiction of the assassination attempt

One of London's most famous criminals wasn't known for the crimes he committed but for the prisons he escaped. Born in 1702, Jack Sheppard grew up as a carpenter's apprentice before running away to become a thief. The year 1724 saw him in his first prison, which he escaped within three hours by cutting through the roof and climbing down a rope made of blankets. Apparently, his knowledge of tools had come in handy, and his future career showed an incredible talent for hiding them on his person and using even the most improbable items to secure his release.

Sheppard

It wasn't long after Sheppard's first escape that he was caught pick-pocketing and sent to prison again. The warders, cautious with a prisoner who had already escaped once, chained him to the wall of his cell, but with a hidden tool, he sawed his way through the metal and then cut through the nine-inch beam that locked his cell door.

Once again he was eventually caught, sentenced to death, and this time sent to Newgate, the most notorious prison in London, feared by criminals all across the city. Doubtless, his jailers searched him, but they missed an iron spike with which he dug through a stone wall and disappeared into the throngs celebrating Bartholomew Fair. He joined the party for a time before getting caught robbing a shop.

By now Sheppard was famous, and his cell at Newgate became a tourist attraction. When some members of the clergy came to preach to him, he sneered, "One file is worth all the Bibles in the world." His words were ill-chosen. The jailers searched him again and found a file. They moved him to a cell on the fifth floor, chained him to the floor, and shackled his hands and legs. But while the jailers had found the file, they missed a small nail. That was all he needed to break free.

He then broke into a chimney that gave him access to an upper room. Finding the door locked from the outside, he used the nail as a lockpick, got into the prison chapel, removed a more suitable spike from one of the railings, used to it unlock four more doors, and made it to the roof.

Sheppard looked at the dizzying drop below him and realized he needed a rope, so he went all the way back to his cell to retrieve his blankets, returned to the roof, tied them together, and shimmied down to freedom.

A depiction of his escape

After going on another crime spree, he dressed himself up in fashionable clothes and hired a carriage to take a ride around town, even stopping at Newgate to drink at the neighboring pubs.

As it turned out, Sheppard's talent for escape was matched by his poor luck, and the constables captured him that same evening. It was back to Newgate for him, this time under constant guard, and soon he was on the road to the gallows at Tyburn. The guards, ever suspicious, searched him for what must have been the 10th time and found a penknife on him. How he got it in the first place when he was under constant watch is a mystery, but it was his last trick. Jack Sheppard was led up to the gallows and into the lore of London.

There are few types of criminal more unpopular than a corrupt policeman, combining as they do dishonesty and hypocrisy, and Jonathan Wild earned the dubious distinction of not only being London's most corrupt cop but also one of the first. Born into poverty in 1682 or 1683, he lived as a minor criminal in London until a change of public policy allowed him to achieve greatness. Crime was on the rise, and only a disorganized patchwork of local constabularies and private bodyguards protected the citizenry. A new post of City Under Marshal was supposed to bring order to this chaos. With authority to make arrests throughout the city, the "thief-taker," as he was popularly called, was a powerful post indeed.

In 1711, Charles Hitchen bought the post with a £700 bribe. Hitchen extorted money from criminals and only arrested those who couldn't or wouldn't pay. In 1713, Jonathan Wild became his assistant and learned all his dirty tricks. Wild soon decided he didn't want to share the wealth and opened his own office, claiming to be Hitchen's deputy. He ran a gang of thieves that would rob houses and then collect a reward for "finding" and returning the goods. His system became so efficient that other thieves gave their loot to him for a portion of the price, knowing they would be safe from persecution for fencing stolen merchandise.

This trust proved to be ill-placed. Wild often sent thieves to the gallows to collect rewards from the government. Hitchen didn't like the competition and denounced him, but Wild alleged, correctly, that Hitchen was a homosexual who got freebies at one of London's most popular gay clubs, known as "molly houses." While Hitchen avoided execution for sodomy, his reputation was ruined.

Wild appeared to be a noble defender of the public morals, but his crime spree could not last. One of Wild's henchmen, the now famous jailbreaker Jack Sheppard, made him look like a fool by escaping half a dozen times from various prisons. The constant accusations and rumors against Wild began to be taken seriously, and when he tried to break one of his associates out of jail (a rare feat for a man who usually sent his friends to jail) he was arrested.

Criminals came to the court in droves to denounce him, and he went to the gallows at Tyburn on May 24, 1725. His execution brought so much public interest that his body was dug up by resurrection men and sold to the Royal College of Surgeons for dissection. His skeleton is now on display at the college's Hunterian Museum.

A ticket to view Wild's hanging

The most famous thief of them all was a mysterious figure named Dick Turpin, whose name is now synonymous with the cavalier highwayman, a gentleman rogue who robbed at will and laughed at the law. However, like many other famous criminals, the reality of his career became superseded by the imagination of the public.

A Victorian Era romanticized depiction of a highway robbery

Turpin was born in 1705 and started his career rather ignobly as a butcher in Whitechapel, then a village on the edge of London. Even in his early days he was less than honest and filled out his larder by stealing cattle and other livestock. This eventually got him charged with stealing two oxen, a crime punishable by death.

Now on the run, he joined the famous "Essex Gang" and roved the countryside of Essex and the outskirts of London poaching the King's deer and raiding isolated houses. By 1735 King George II had put a price of 50 pounds on their heads.

The gang's most notorious crime was raiding the country home of a rich old widow in Essex. When the woman refused to reveal where she had hidden her money, they threatened to roast her in her own hearth. This got them £700 in loot, but foolishly they then moved into a tavern in Westminster and spent their time getting drunk. The police surprised them in their cups, captured most of them, and sent them to the gallows, except for Turpin, who managed to escape out a window.

Turpin apparently didn't learn from his brush with death and continued his career as a robber, using Epping Forest as his base of operations. He robbed hundreds of stagecoaches and travelers, and by 1737 the price on his head had gone up to 100 pounds, a handsome sum in those days. Sometime in this period, Turpin made his greatest haul yet, a thoroughbred horse named "Black Bess." She could outrun any horse the police or soldiers rode, and the horse helped him get out of numerous scrapes, but the original owner wanted her back and set up numerous wanted posters around London describing Turpin and Black Bess. When Turpin's partner in crime Tom King went to fetch Black Bess for Turpin at a stable in Whitechapel, he found the constables waiting for him. Turpin rushed to save King, but in the ensuing gunfight he accidentally shot and killed him. He did retrieve Black Bess, however, and is said to have ridden off to York, a distance of 200 miles, in 15 hours. This is patently impossible; in fact, the story was lifted from a tale about an earlier highwayman who couldn't possibly have achieved the feat either.

A penny dreadful about Black Bess

However much time it actually took, Turpin did escape to Yorkshire and set himself up as a horse dealer, filling his stables the same way he filled his butcher shop. He was eventually arrested for this, and the judge discovered his real identity. Never convicted of his highway robberies, Turpin went to the gallows for horse theft in 1739.

It was only in his final hours that this lowly thief became the noble rogue of legend. He hired five mourners to accompany his cart to the gallows, and while on the platform he treated the crowd to a florid speech for a full half hour before the rope was put around his neck and Dick Turpin, after chatting pleasantly with the hangman and constables, leaped off the platform and hanged himself.

London's main place of execution, Tyburn, was for many years the biggest attraction in the city, a place to take the family and enjoy a good show and forget about life's troubles for a while. Because what could be more fun than seeing some people slowly hanged to death? If one was lucky, he or she might see 24 criminals all hanged at the same time!

"Tyburn" referred to a row of elm trees next to Tyburn Brook, which like most of London's streams is now hidden in an underground culvert. Criminals were hanged from these trees from at least the year 1196, when William Longbeard became the first recorded execution. It soon became London's favorite place of execution and became busier as the city grew. Mondays would be the usual day of execution, and large crowds would gather around, whether sitting on temporary bleachers or renting space in windows overlooking the place of execution.

Then as today, executions were surrounded with certain rituals. The condemned would be taken out of Newgate Prison on an open cart so all could see them. Prisoners would spare no expense to dress up for the occasion and tried their best to maintain a calm and cool demeanor, knowing their every move and word would be reported in the broadsides and newspapers of the day. The cart would slowly move down Snow Hill accompanied by large crowds, across Holborn Bridge, down Broad Street, along Oxford Street to finally stop at Tyburn.

On the way, the condemned would stop at a pub for a final drink. Once they were finished, they would have to "get back on the wagon" and never drink again. This might be the origin of the popular expression.

Once at the gallows, those about to die would be allowed to address the crowd. Many would repent of their sins and make florid speeches on how crime doesn't pay. Others boasted of their misdeeds and thumbed their nose at the executioners. One suspects these speeches might have gone on for quite a long time as the speakers would certainly have been in no rush to finish. The location of the Tyburn Tree was around Mable Arch, quite close to where Speakers' Corner in Hyde Park is today. It's thought that the tradition of anyone being allowed to speak their mind to the public at Speakers' Corner originated with the speeches of the condemned at Tyburn.

In 1571, in response to growing demand, the authorities erected a giant Tyburn Tree, a triangular scaffold that could accommodate up to 24 people at once. The criminals would be lined up on a long cart, the nooses tied around their necks, and then the cart would be driven away. This would leave the victims dangling in the air, their legs gyrating wildly in the "dead man's dance." More modern hangings feature a long drop so the neck broke and the criminal died quickly, but this was not so with the Tyburn Tree. As soon as the cart drove off, friends and relatives of the condemned would rush forward and yank on the dying person's legs to snap their neck. Others would rush forward too, but they did so in order to grab bits of hair, nails, or clothing to keep as mementos or to use in black magic. Once the bodies had been manhandled in this manner, the surgeons might take them away for dissection. Only criminals of the worst sort were condemned to dissection.

A medieval depiction of the "Tyburn Tree"

Samuel Johnson, who compiled the first authoritative dictionary in the English language, understood why these grisly displays were permitted. They were meant as a method of educating the public of the power of the law and giving the criminal a last chance at redemption. Johnson told his biographer James Boswell, "Sir, executions are intended to draw spectators. If they don't draw spectators, they don't answer their purpose…The public was gratified by a procession: the criminal was supported by it."

Sadly, not all those who were executed at Tyburn were bad people. During the Protestant Reformation brought on by Henry VIII, Catholicism was outlawed. People caught practicing the

Catholic religion could be faced with the death penalty, and countless Catholics were strung up on the Tyburn Tree for no crime except following their faith.

Executions continued at Tyburn until John Austin became the last person to be hanged there in 1783. After that, the executions were moved to Newgate Prison, likely because neighbors and businesses had complained that the large crowds at Tyburn had gotten out of hand.

Odd Old Professions

The previous section may make one think that Londoners of yore never did a respectable day's work, but in reality, most people in that great city worked honestly and worked hard. Some of them worked in professions that have long since disappeared, and their job descriptions explain much about early life in the city.

One such profession was the ale-conner, who was responsible for keeping up standards on alcoholic drinks, especially ale. Given the famous English love of ale, the ale-conner held an important position. It was a yearly post, and four men would be appointed by the Livery Companies, an early form of trade union, in their common hall on Midsummer Day. The ale-conner's duties included checking on the quality and price and measures of bread, ale, and all liquors. He had the authority to impose fines, making him unpopular with the pub landlords, and he had to taste samples from every public house in the city.

Believe it or not, this wasn't as fun of a job as it sounds. Hops weren't introduced to the recipe until the end of the 14th century by Flemish immigrants, meaning that throughout most of the Middle Ages the brew consisted of only of malt, yeast, and water. This resulted in a strong, sickly sweet drink that quickly went off. It could also give people food poisoning.

With hops in the recipe, the brew had to be boiled, which killed off the bacteria, making a safer drink that lasted longer. Thus in the early days before hops, public houses brewed their own and often kept it long past its expiration date.

As a result, the ale-conner had to sample the wares from each pub, downing some pretty bad brew in the course of his duties and running the possibility of sickness or even death. There are numerous records from early London demonstrating that ale-conners were often fined for not performing their duties. One widespread tale is that the ale-conner tested the quality of ale by pouring some on a wooden bench and sitting on it. How much it stuck to his specially made leather trousers determined its quality. However, this appears to be a myth.

A more famous profession was the chimney sweep. Before gas heating, Londoners heated their homes and cooked their meals on open fireplaces. Every rooftop had a chimney, and the skyline was a haze of wood and coal smoke. City law required homeowners to keep their chimneys clean because a buildup of soot could be a fire hazard. Not all the material that gets blown up a flue is inert, and if enough builds up, the chimney could catch fire, destroying the house and even entire neighborhoods. The Great Fire of London in 1666 destroyed more than 13,000 homes and left the majority of Londoners without shelter. Thus the humble chimney sweep performed an essential task, although like a lot of essential jobs, it was looked down on as menial and paid accordingly.

Chimney sweeps started their career at age 7 or 8 as "climbing boys" apprenticed to a master sweep. Their task was to climb up the flue to clean out anything the master sweep couldn't reach. Many died of suffocation or black lung, and those who survived a few years often grew up deformed or developed scrotum cancer, a product of being constantly covered in soot.

However, while they had a dirty and dangerous job, chimney sweeps captured the public imagination. They ran across rooftops while the rest of the population was packed into busy streets. Moreover, despite being poor, they had access to the wealthiest homes in the city. Once a year they were honored in the May Day celebrations, along with another menial laborer, the milk maid.

Lower down on the social scale was the mudlark. A popular job for poor boys in the 18th and 19th centuries, the mudlark scoured the banks of the Thames for items of value. These could be anything, from lost coins, lumps of coal, and bits of metal to cloth that could be sold for scrap. The Thames in those days was busy with boats and construction, so there would be quite a lot of detritus for the hardworking mudlark to pick up. They could be seen every day when the tides were low, picking through the river's muddy banks looking for items to scavenge.

Social reformer Henry Mayhew interviewed a 13 year old mudlark for his 1861 book *London Labour and the London Poor; Extra Volume*. The boy, who Mayhew didn't name, had this to say:

> "About two years ago I left school, and commenced to work as a mudlark on the river, in the neighbourhood of Millwall, picking up pieces of coal and iron, and copper, and bits of canvas on the bed of the river, or of wood floating on the surface…

> "When the bargemen heave coals to be carried from their barge to the shore, pieces drop into the water among the mud, which we afterwards pick up. Sometimes we get as many coals about one barge as sell for 6d. On other occasions we work for days, and only get perhaps as much as sells for 6d…

> "We often find among the mud, in the bed of the river, pieces of iron; such as rivets out of ships, and what is termed washers and other articles cast away or dropped in the iron-yards in building ships and barges. We get these in the neighbourhood of Limehouse, where they build boats and vessels. I generally get some pieces of iron every day, which sells at ¼d. a pound and often make 1d. or 2d.

a day, sometimes 3d., at other times only a farthing. Pieces of rope are occasionally dropped or thrown overboard from the ships or barges and are found embedded in the mud. Rope is sold to the marine store dealers at ½d. a pound. We also get pieces of canvas, which sells at ½d. a pound. I have on some occasions got as much as three pounds. We also pick up pieces of fat along the river-side. Sometimes we get four or five pounds and sell it at ¾d. a pound at the marine stores; these are thrown overboard by the cooks in the ships, and after floating on the river are driven on shore.

"…Some of the mudlarks are orphan boys and have no home. In the summer time they often sleep in the barges or in sheds or stables or cow-houses, with their clothes on. Some of them have not a shirt, others have a tattered shirt which is never washed, as they have no father nor mother, nor friend to care for them. Some of these orphan lads have good warm clothing; others are ragged and dirty, and covered with vermin.

"…The Thames' police often come upon us and carry off our bags and baskets with the contents. The mudlarks are generally good swimmers. When a bargeman gets hold of them in his barge on the river, he often throws them into the river, when they swim ashore and take off their wet clothes and dry them. They are often seized by the police in the middle of the river, and thrown overboard, when they swim to the shore. I have been chased twice by a police galley."

An even more miserable variety of mudlark was the tosher, who specialized in scouring London's sewer system for any valuables dropped out of the pockets of squatting citizens. Toshers were a later development since London didn't even have a citywide sewer system until Joseph Bazalgette developed one after the Great Stink of 1858. What few sewers London did have had gradually backed up until, during the hot summer of 1858, the stench got so bad that many people fled town. Famed novelist Charles Dickens wrote, "I can certify that the offensive smells, even in that short whiff, have been of a most head-and-stomach-distending nature." The sewer system Bazalgette designed was a masterpiece of Victorian engineering and still serves London to this day.

Bazalgette

Besides mudlarking, there was another job mostly performed by young boys. For much of its history, London had no street lighting, so while the citizens of Baghdad could walk home under the light of oil lamps as early as the Middle Ages, Londoners were in the dark until the late 19th century. This created work for young boys who knew the streets and weren't afraid to venture out at night. The linkboy, as they were called, was a young boy, usually an orphan or one whose parents were so desperate for money that they would allow their child to roam London's benighted streets, who would offer his services as a guide. He would carry a lantern on a pole and would loiter around theatres and taverns hoping for customers, much like the coachmen of a later era. For a few pennies, they would take drunken Londoners or lost visitors to their home or hotel.

London's winding streets are difficult enough to navigate in the days of electricity and street signs, but in the past, with no signs, no lights, and thick fog on many nights, it was well-nigh impossible for anyone but a sober local to make it safely from one point to another. Linkboys could also be relied upon to show their customers to bawdy houses, getting a cut from the madame in addition to their tip.

Of course, the job of linkboy relied on trust, and that trust was often broken. The wise traveler would hold off paying until he was safely shown to his destination, or else the linkboy might grab his tuppence and disappear in the fog. Even this precaution didn't save everyone, because linkboys sometimes teamed up with robbers and would steer their customers down remote alleyways where they'd be set upon. Everyone knew this, but little could be done; the linkboys provided an essential service, and the trusted ones would often be called upon night after night. Their bobbing lanterns were a common sight in early London.

In the early 19th century, cheap printing and a rise in disposable income led to a boom in advertising. Soon every wall was covered in posters, and the streets became filled with "sandwich men," poorly paid fellows drawn from the city's indigent to serve as mobile advertisements, their front and back covered with boards held up by ropes over their shoulders. The term comes from a quip by Dickens describing one as a "piece of human flesh sandwiched between two slices of pasteboard."

The sandwich men wore a variety of elaborate costumes or fine clothes, usually borrowed from their wealthy employers, and had to stand out in the sun and rain for up to 12 hours advertising every product imaginable. A sketch from the 1830s shows a little boy wearing a sandwich board in the shape of a turtle shell, advertising Port wine. The novelty soon wore off, and advertisers had to come up with more outlandish ways to capture the public attention. Some sent out legions of sandwich men to walk in a long procession. Others blew trumpets or tossed gifts to the crowd. A shoe polish company even sent out a line of men dressed in giant tins of shoe polish.

Other companies decided bigger was better and made giant carts covered in huge ads that trundled down the streets, blocking traffic. The satirical magazine *Punch* joked that the ads were so big that a person could only read half a letter at a time, and the carts proved such a nuisance that they were banned under the London Hackney Carriage Act of 1853.

Nonetheless, the sandwich man survived the new law, as he was not deemed a sufficient hazard to traffic. The position survived the invention of the radio and neon too, and only fell out of fashion in the 1960s, although they are occasionally revived as a gimmick. There's been a rise in recent years of sandwich men as well as people holding giant signs on the end of a pole in a desperate attempt to be seen through the heaving throngs of London's busy shopping districts.

Only in the 21st century have their days finally come to a true end. The Westminster City Council banned them in 2008, mostly in a bid to increase "shopping ambiance" in the popular

West End. It remains to be seen whether other boroughs will follow suit, or if the ban can last.

Magicians and Witches

Before the development of modern science, inquiring minds sought knowledge in some strange ways. Alchemy tried to understand the building blocks of the natural world through the analysis and mixture of various substances. While in many ways alchemy was the predecessor to modern chemistry, the field included a hefty dose of religion and mysticism.

Alchemy is best known for its relentless quest for the Philosopher's Stone, a fabled substance that could turn base metals into gold. The more perceptive members of the craft saw this as a metaphor for spiritual enlightenment, a purification of the soul in the fire of truth, but alchemy attracted more than its fair share of cranks who thought they could strike it rich if they could only discover the correct formula. In dirty back alleys and sumptuous drawing rooms, there arose strange odors as generations of alchemists mixed every substance imaginable in their quest. A 17th century painting by Adriaen van Ostade titled "An Alchemist" in London's National Gallery satirizes this craze by showing an obsessive alchemist working at his fireplace while ignoring his wife, who stands in the background taking care of their child in their impoverished home.

If anything, the only people who got rich off of alchemy were hucksters. Traveling salesmen would hawk narwhal tusks as unicorn horns, or the sap from the Dragon Tree in the Canary Islands as dragon's blood. The more exotic the substance, the more extravagant the price, since surely the Philosopher's Stone would be made up of the rarest of magical ingredients. In the Enlightenment Gallery of the British Museum, there's a steel penknife with a tip of pure gold. The craftsmen who created this item used it to show that he had discovered the Philosopher's Stone, his proof being that he had dipped the point of the knife into the substance and it had turned to gold. He would reveal his secret for a fee, and apparently no one questioned why the discoverer of alchemy's greatest secret would need money.

Even the rapid advance of real science in the 17th century didn't end alchemy's hold over the public's imagination, but leading scientists felt compelled to hide their magical studies behind the anonymity of pseudonyms. Jeova Sanctus Unus was one of a close group of London astrologers and magicians that made up the "Invisible College." He wrote extensively on the mystical arts, but he was also one of the century's greatest mathematicians and physicists. Jeova and other members of the Invisible College founded the Royal Society, one of the first scientific societies in the world, which is still today a leading force in the advancement of science, and the Royal Society reveres Jeova Sanctus Unus as one of their founders, albeit under his better-known name: Sir Isaac Newton.

Newton

In the days before the city streets were lit by gas lamps, Londoners could still study the stars, and perhaps not surprisingly, early Londoners were fascinated by the concept that the heavens controlled the future. A glance at the back pages of many London newspapers will show that not too much has changed.

While astrology is often mocked in today's world, it had an even harder time in the past. The Church equated astrology with magic and proclaimed that only God could know and control the future. In the Middle Ages, astrologers could be burned at the stake, though in later times they were merely imprisoned, a punishment only slightly less lethal considering the conditions of the prisons of the time. In 1561, an astrologer named Hugh Draper was imprisoned in the Salt Tower of the Tower of London, and the complex horoscope he scratched on the wall can still be seen.

By the next century, astrology was enjoying its height of popularity, brought on by a more permissive Church and the widespread distribution of printed pamphlets. During the English Civil War, William Lilly became famous when his pamphlet predicted the Roundheads would win the battle of Naseby in 1645. Another prominent astrologer, George Wharton, predicted the Royalists would win and thereby ruined his reputation.

Astrologers and other practitioners of the magical arts congregated around the Seven Dials, an intersection of seven streets in Camden. In an interesting example of London's continuity of place, nearby Neal Street houses the city's largest astrology center.

Strange English Creatures

Mankind has always been fascinated with the hidden, the mysterious, and the unexplained. Every society has its tall tales and ghost stories, its odd legends and heroes. Also, every society has its stories of strange beasts, dangerous or benign, that live in the twilight world between the everyday and the legendary. Through most of history people have been closely tied to nature, hunting in forests and having an intimate knowledge of the animals in our region. So-called "primitive" peoples were walking encyclopedias of the natural world, and yet most believed there were more creatures lurking in those woods than the ones they usually encountered.

Given how long people have lived on the land, it is no surprise England is filled with tales of strange beasts. Of course, there have always been tales of mythical animals in England—the mermaids and the dragons, the unicorns and the wild men—but even in the modern era people continue to see strange creatures unknown to science. Reports are so persistent in England and around the world that it has created a whole field of study called cryptozoology.

Cryptozoology is the science that investigates as yet unconfirmed creatures, which investigators generally call "cryptids." The word is made up of the Greek stem "kryptos" (hidden) and suffix "zoology" (study of animals), thus cryptozoology is the study of hidden, as-yet-undiscovered animals. It is important to be precise in our definition because there is a great deal of popular misconception of what cryptozoology is and what cryptozoologists do.

Contrary to popular opinion, cryptozoologists do not study the paranormal. They are not ghost hunters or ufologists. While many cryptozoologists are interested in such phenomena, their own work focuses on finding flesh and blood animals that have not been discovered by science. Visitors from other planets or from beyond the grave do not concern them. Some of the leading researchers are themselves scientists, with advanced degrees in zoology or biology, and yet reject mainstream science's assumption that all large species have already been discovered and catalogued. Other cryptozoologists are not so careful, and the field is sadly filled with a large number of credulous, sloppy researchers.

Cryptozoology is also hampered by the fact that there have been so many hoaxes, to the extent that the study is often scoffed at and widely considered a pseudoscience. But one of the reasons it made men like P.T. Barnum rich and continues to fascinate people today is the fact that people realize they've only scratched the surface when it comes to identifying all the different forms of life on Earth. As Martin DelRio explained in *The Loch Ness Monster*, "Could ... an undiscovered animal as large as the Loch Ness monster possibly exist? The answer is yes. Animals previously unknown to science have been found more than once in the past hundred years. For instance, there's the megamouth shark (megachasma pelagios), a fifteen-foot-long creature weighing nearly a ton. The first specimen was discovered on November 15, 1976, when it was found entangled in the drag anchor of a U.S. Navy ship. The new creature wasn't described scientifically until 1983 ... The megamouth remains the only species in its genus, and the only genus in its order."

Cryptozoologists range from gullible cranks to trained zoologists and biologists respected in their more mainstream fields, and while some of their reports must be taken with a grain of salt, there are enough serious researchers in the field to make it worthy of a look. In England, the most common cryptids are so-called Alien Big Cats, which cryptozoologists affectionately refer to as ABCs. Alien Big Cats aren't monsters, and they certainly aren't aliens in the sense of coming from UFOs. Instead, they appear to be known species such as tigers, pumas, and panthers found in places they shouldn't be—like England. Large predators have been extinct in England for centuries, but there are persistent sightings of large felines and even some enigmatic tracks and other physical evidence.

The most famous English ABC is the Beast of Bodmin Moor. This bleak moor in Cornwall in the extreme southwest of England is one of England's largest at 80 square miles, but much of it is sparsely inhabited. The stunning terrain of bleak wetlands and rugged granite hills has given rise to a number of legends. For example, Dozmary Pool, a small lake on the moor, is said to be the one where Sir Bedivere threw Excalibur to The Lady of the Lake after the death of King Arthur.

Phillip Capper's picture of Bodmin Moor

Dozmary Pool

In this wild and forbidding landscape, hikers and farmers have frequently spotted a large, black feline that some say resembles a panther. Most reports agree that it measures about five feet long and has yellow eyes. The sightings started in 1983, and soon dozens of reports flooded in to local police and wildlife organizations. In 1995, the government launched an investigation into the beast, but investigators found no proof of any large feline living in the moor.

Just a week after the release of the government report, cryptozoologists thought they had the smoking gun when a 14 year old boy discovered a strange skull in the waters of the River Fowey. It measured four inches by seven inches and had two long canines like many predators. The lower jaw was missing, but the rest of the skull was well preserved. It was sent to the Natural History Museum in London for analysis, and the scientists there said it came from a young male leopard.

Unfortunately for believers in the Beast of Bodmin Moor, that wasn't all they said. They discovered that the back of the skull had been cut away by a metal tool, and that the skull had scrapes on it, indicating that it had been defleshed with a knife. Inside the skull the researchers found the egg case of a tropical cockroach that doesn't live in England. Ultimately, the lab concluded that the skull was part of a leopard rug imported to England from Africa. The good level of preservation indicated that it hadn't been in the water long, suggesting that it had been thrown there after being pulled off the rug and having its flesh removed in order to provide "evidence" to contradict the government report. Some practical joker, or someone interested in continuing the legend to attract tourists, had tried to pull one over on the believing public.

Nevertheless, that ruse did not stop the sightings. In 1998, a local captured the beast on video. Judging from the background, the black feline appeared to be about three and a half feet long, far bigger than a housecat. This prompted local Member of Parliament Paul Tyler to submit the video and other reports as evidence supporting the need for a new investigation. His request was ignored.

Keith Edkins' picture of Paul Tyler

Other Alien Big Cats prowl different regions of England, and sightings are so common that many local governments have launched investigations and a national network of specialists log and investigate reports. These creatures are by far the most common cryptid to be seen in England.

Several skulls have been found of large feline predators, including a puma skull discovered by a farmer in Devon in July 2005. Unlike the Bodmin Moor skull, these skulls were not removed from rugs, and scientists have no explanation for how they ended up in England. Numerous tracks consistent with pumas and panthers have been found, photographed, and cast with plaster. Indirect evidence for Alien Big Cats has also come in the form of attacks on livestock, especially sheep and horses. These poor animals are often killed and partially eaten, or left badly injured with severe claw marks.

The British Big Cats Society, which collects reports on ABCs in England, Scotland, and Wales, logs more than a thousand sightings a year. For England, the most popular place is the southwest, including Cornwall, Devon, and Somerset. The society tends to avoid theorizing on what the ABCs are, preferring to focus on gathering evidence, but they do point out that the Dangerous Animals Act of 1976 was passed just before a growing trend in ABC sightings. This act forbade the keeping of various wild animals, including feline predators such as panthers, pumas, and lynxes, the most common types of cats spotted. *BBC Science* investigated the issue and found 23 cases of exotic animal owners who had kept large feline predators after they had been banned and who then got scared and released them into the wild.

As a result, real, and really illegal, cats can explain some of the sightings, but can they explain all? There have been so many reports from across the United Kingdom over the years that it would require a huge underground network of illegal pet owners to be constantly releasing their animals into the wild.

While the English have a well-known fondness for cats, they have more than their fair share of mysterious dogs prowling the countryside too. These tend not to be physical creatures, but more along the lines of spirits or ghosts. These huge black dogs, some as big as a horse, have glowing red eyes and are almost always seen at night. Some say they are the Devil's dogs, and call them hellhounds.

While they tend not to directly attack people, they are a sign of disaster and death. Sightings follow a similar pattern. A lone traveler will be passing along a crossroads or a place of execution at night and will see the dog cross his path. It won't be long until the traveler or one of his kinfolk dies.

Others only seem to be passive ghosts, like the one that allegedly haunts the road at Tring, Hertfordshire. Known as the Lean Dog, he is the ghost of a chimney sweep hanged for murder at the gibbet that once stood on the spot. People passing by this stretch of road at night have spotted a large, lean black dog with glowing eyes standing in the middle of the road. If the traveler is brave enough to approach the apparition, the dog sinks into the earth and disappears.

One of the most common places for strange sightings is the Island of Man, an island in the Irish Sea located between Scotland, England, Ireland, and Wales that has a strange status. It is not part of the United Kingdom or even the European Union; instead, it is an independently administered possession of the British Crown. The Manx are British citizens but not part of England.

On the Isle of Man, people whisper of the Moddey Dhoo, which means "black dog" in Manx, the local variety of Gaelic. It tends to lurk around Peel Castle but can be seen further abroad. Anyone who sees it will die soon after. In his history of the Isle of Man, George Waldron described the Moddey Dhoo: "They say, that an apparition called, in their language, the Mauthe Doog, in the shape of a large black spaniel with curled shaggy hair, was used to haunt Peel Castle; and has been frequently seen in every room, but particularly in the guard-chamber, where, as soon as candles were lighted, it came and lay down before the fire in presence of all the soldiers, who at length, by being so much accustomed to the sight of it, lost great part of the terror they were seized with at its first appearance."

Peel Castle is one of the great attractions of the Isle of Man. Its origins reach all the way back to Viking times, when it was the fort of Magnus Barefoot, the 11th century Viking King of Mann. The ruins include an 10th century round tower and church dedicated to St Patrick Church, and an eerie 13th century crypt of the now abandoned Cathedral of St German. The gatehouse tower, where guards used to keep watch over the land and sea, became the scene for one of the many sightings of the Moddey Dhoo. It was there during the reign of King Charles II (1660-85) that the guards began seeing the spectral hound lounging every night by the guardhouse fire or wandering the darkened halls of the castle. No one dared approach it, and the guards always kept each other company on their rounds, nervously gripping their spears and looking into every shadow, fearful of seeing a baleful pair of red eyes looking back at them.

Peel Castle

Kevin Rothwell's picture of the cathedral

One night, a soldier got drunk, as soldiers frequently do, and got to bragging that he was braver than his comrades. Lounging in the guardhouse, he gestured over to the mysterious dog sitting by the fire and declared that he wasn't afraid of it. It was time to take the castle key to the Captain of the Guard, and he said he would take it alone. If the dog followed him, well, maybe he could clear up the mystery of whether it was a devil or simply an unusually large dog.

Off he staggered, key in hand. A minute later, the Moddey Dhoo got up and went off after him. The guards stared in wonder, and none volunteered to go after their friend to warn him. Suddenly, horrible screams echoed through the castle. The guards, pale with fear, didn't dare budge from the guardhouse. A few minutes later, their drunken colleague stumbled back into the room. He wouldn't say a word. He merely sat there shaking, his eyes bugging out. Three days later, he died without ever revealing what happened to him in the dark halls of Peel Castle.

The waters around the Isle of Man are also filled with strange beasts. One is the Beisht Kione, which means "the beast with the black head" in Manx. Descriptions are vague, since any fisherman who spotted its black head rising above the surface of the sea sailed away as fast as they could, but it appears to have been a typical sea serpent found in all the waters of the world.

Then there is the Cabyll-Ushtey, the Manx water horse. In fact, the Cabyll-Ushtey is considered a regional monster, known as the Each Uisge in Scotland and the Aughisky in Ireland. This pale gray creature looks just like a regular horse, except that it lives in the water and eats man and beast alike. One unfortunate farmer at Kerro Clough kept losing cows, and he suspected the Cabyll-Ushtey was taking them. Sure enough, one day he saw the mystical horse come up out of the water and carry off one of his herd. He moved his herd to different grazing ground away from water, but he failed to move his own residence and the Cabyll-Ushtey, frustrated at losing his regular diet of beef, took the farmer's daughter.

Another beast is the water bull, a strange magical bull that lives in the sea but will occasionally come onto land to mingle with the herds and lure away cows. Apparently the water bull was more attractive, in the bovine sense, than normal bulls. In his 1844 book, *A History of the Isle of Man*, Joseph Train gives an account of the creature: "A neighbour of mine who kept cattle, had his fields very much infested with this animal, by which he had lost several cows; he therefore placed a man continually to watch, who bringing him word one day that a strange bull was among the cows, he doubted not that it was the Water-bull, and having called a good number of lusty men to his assistance, who were all armed with great poles, pitchforks, and other weapons proper to defend themselves of this dangerous enemy; they went to the place where they were told he was, and run altogether at him, but he was too nimble for their pursuit, and after tiring them over mountains and rocks and a great space of stony ground, he took a river and avoided any further chase, by diving down into it, though every now and then he would show his head above water, as if to mock their skill."

Up in York in northeast England, a spectral black dog can sometimes be seen on the back roads, or even around Clifford's Tower, the colloquial name for York Castle, the imposing Norman castle that sits atop an artificial mound in the center of the city. He is said to bring disaster on anyone so unfortunate as to see it. Perhaps he is a vengeful spirit from the city's greatest crime. In 1190, the citizens of York rioted against the local Jewish community. The riot was said to have been started by a man who was in debt to a Jewish moneylender and decided that mass murder was a more appealing option than repayment. The terrified Jews fled to the castle and the warden let them in, shutting the stout gate behind them. The warden then went out to speak with the mob. The parley didn't achieve much and when he tried to reenter the gate, the Jews wouldn't open it for him, fearing the mob would charge in with him. The frustrated warden then called out the York militia and besieged his own castle. After a long fight the militia managed to set the tower on fire and the Jews, caught between the options of burning to death or being savaged by the mob, decided to kill themselves. About 500 died. For many years afterwards, on the anniversary of the tragedy, the walls would glow red at night as a grim reminder to the guilty citizens of York of their evil deeds.

M. Koolman's picture of York Castle

England's most famous spectral black dog is Black Shuck of East Anglia. It's most often seen in the fens, fields, and back roads of Norfolk, Suffolk, Essex, and Cambridgeshire. Accounts of his appearance vary, with some saying he has two glowing red eyes, while others claim he only has one in the center of his head. Some say he has no head at all and sits on a floating cloud above the ground. All agree, however, that he's terrifying.

Terrifying, but not always harmful. While some have died after seeing Black Shuck, or had kinsmen die, the creature is a gentleman and makes sure lone women make it home unmolested.

One would think that this is merely a local folktale, something to scare the superstitious on long winter's nights, except that a large number of people once saw Black Shuck appear in church. The incident was recorded in a pamphlet called *A Straunge and Terrible Wunder*, written in 1577 by the Reverend Abraham Fleming. He relates that on August 4, 1577, at St Mary's Church, Bungay, Black Shuck decided to visit: "This black dog, or the divel in such a linenesse (God hee knoweth al who worketh all,) running all along down the body of the church with great swiftnesse, and incredible haste, among the people, in a visible fourm and shape, passed between two persons, as they were kneeling uppon their knees, and occupied in prayer as it seemed, wrung the necks of them bothe at one instant clene backward, in somuch that even at a mome[n]t where they kneeled, they stra[n]gely dyed."

That same day, the parishioners at Holy Trinity Church at Blythburgh, Suffolk were holding services when they heard a clap of thunder. Black Shuck appeared and ran up the nave past the startled assembly. The church steeple collapsed, driving right through the roof and killing two of the congregation. Before he left, Black Shuck pressed his hellish paws against the north door and left scorch marks that can still be seen to this day. Locally they're called "the Devil's fingerprints" because at the time of his appearance, Black Shuck was considered the Devil in dog form.

A straunge

and terrible Wunder wrought very late in the parish Church of Bongay, a Towne of no great distance from the citie of Norwich, namely the fourth of this August, in ye yeere of our Lord 1577. in a great tempest of violent raine, lightning, and thunder, the like whereof hath been sel= dome seene.

With the apperance of an horrible shaped thing, sensibly perceiued of the people then and there assembled.

Drawen into a plain method ac= cording to the written coppe. by Abraham Fleming.

A 16th century depiction of Black Shuck

While Alien Big Cats and black dogs are most common south of the border with Scotland, England seems to be vying with its northern neighbor as the home for lake monsters. In fact, even in modern times people have spotted odd things in the water. For example, in 1961, there was a wave of mermaid sightings, and they were so frequent that the Manx Tourism Board offered a reward if anyone could catch the mermaid. There were no takers.

The Loch Ness Monster will always be the most famous, but a few English lakes have their own mysteries lurking beneath the water. In Cumbria's beautiful Lake District National Park lies Windermere, the largest natural lake in England at almost six square miles. It's the perfect setting for a monster. Locals speak of a long-necked creature much like the one in Loch Ness to the north, and they have affectionately dubbed it "Bownessie."

M. Konikkara's picture of Windermere

It's different in one respect, however. While the many lake monsters in Scotland have been talked about for centuries, Bownessie was first spotted in 2006. It was then that journalism lecturer Steve Burnip reported seeing a 30-ft long serpentine creature swimming in the water near Wray Castle. It undulated vertically, creating a series of humps, as is typical with many lake monsters (eels and water snakes, it should be noted, undulate from side to side and do not make humps in the water). A few more sightings have occurred in later years, including one by retired vicar Colin Honour and his wife Christine in 2012, who saw something swimming in the water, making three distinct humps measuring some 20 feet in length. The day was clear and the water was calm, so they got a good look at whatever it was before it slipped under the surface.

James Hopgrove's picture of Wray Castle

In 2014, petrophysicist Matt Benefield snapped a photo of the strange wake that the creature left behind it. Another photo of Bownessie taken by an eyewitness shows a series of humps in the water, but as with so many of this sort of image, it's a bit blurry and indistinct. Of course, local businesses have embraced Bownessie, and while it hasn't led to a tourist boom like anything at Loch Ness, it sure isn't hurting sales.

Another lake monster can allegedly be found in Bassenthwaite Lake, also in northern England's lake district. This lake is four miles long, three-quarters of a mile wide, and some 70 feet deep, making plenty of room for an unknown creature to hide.

Then there's the mystery of Martin Mere, a 17 acre lake in a quiet nature reserve in Lancashire. Unlike many other lakes, Martin Mere doesn't have an old legend attached to it regarding a monster. It seems that whatever is in there is a new arrival. Starting in 1998, swans began disappearing from the lake. A few eyewitnesses claimed to have seen some creature come up from beneath the water and pull the swans below the surface, but it barely broke the surface and moved so quickly that no one could describe it in detail. A few people caught glimpses of a slick black creature "the size of a small car." Soon rumors were flying back and forth, fueled by an eager local press in this usually sleepy region. People bandied about all sorts of theories from giant eels to pikes to mermaids and even dragons.

In 2002, a team from the Centre for Fortean Zoology in Exeter, which specializes in cryptozoology, studied the lake. During their four-day vigil, one of the investigators spotted something black and shiny swimming around near where locals had seen it previously. It had oily skin, and while no one got a good look, the team theorized that it could be a giant Wels catfish from Eastern Europe. This alien species has been introduced into English waters in recent years and can grow to an impressive size. The biggest ever logged was 16 feet, but the team thought the one in Martin Mere could be as little as 7 feet, given the small size of the lake.

Dieter Florian's picture of a Wels catfish

That's still a pretty big fish, and it would need to be. Swans, despite their reputation, are actually rather strong, violent creatures, and a fully grown swan like those seen being yanked under the water can weigh up to 29 pounds. It would take an aggressive fish, or perhaps Nessie on vacation, to do away with one.

Giant catfish have been suggested to explain other water monster sightings, such as in the River Nene, Cambridgeshire, in 2002, and in the Thames in 2016. The Thames monster is especially intriguing since it's in a tidal river running through the United Kingdom's biggest city. Several videos of the creature have emerged on YouTube showing a dark hump rising out of the water for a few seconds before disappearing into the murky water again.

Fatbergs

No discussion of England's stranger side would be complete without mentioning the fearsome fatberg. It's not a cryptid, or an alien, and it would be really, really nice if it was only a folktale, but unfortunately fatbergs are as real as Queen Elizabeth, and every bit as English.

A fatberg is a congealed mass of grease, fat, sanitary wipes, and other items that will not decay in the sewer. Fat, especially cooking fat, may be liquid when it's warm and going down the drain, but it congeals quickly when it reaches the cold sewers. There it sticks to sanitary wipes and other objects, and soon you it creates a blockage.

They have become a problem in recent years, especially in London, where aging sewer systems struggle to keep up with the tons of trash thrown into them on a daily basis. The English eat a lot of fatty foods, including fish and chips, burgers, and the worst of all, kebabs. All this gets balled up into lumps that can become truly astonishing in size. Again and again, English newspapers have trumpeted that the "biggest fatberg ever" has been discovered, only for the record to be broken shortly thereafter. Thames Water spends about £12 million ($16 million) a year getting rid of blockages, and an increasing number of them are caused by fatbergs.

In August of 2013, Thames Water reported a fatberg the size of a bus in the drains beneath London Road in Kingston upon Thames. It was discovered because locals complained to the agency that their toilets weren't flushing. Sewer workers estimated that it weighed some 15 tons, and while they cleared it in time to keep sewage from backing up into neighborhood sinks and toilets, the weight of the fatberg damaged the sewer lines and repairs took six weeks.

In September of the following year, an even bigger fatberg was discovered in a 260 foot section of sewer line beneath Shepherd's Bush. This one was the size of a Boeing 747 and took four days to clear with high-powered hoses. Engineers estimated that it weighed several tons.

In April of 2015, a 10 ton fatberg broke a sewer line beneath the exclusive neighborhood of Chelsea, causing £400,000 ($530,000) in damage.

Needless to say, fatbergs have become a hit on YouTube, but readers who dare to watch those videos should have a strong stomach. People who see the fatbergs often swear off kebabs for life.

While fatbergs may not carry off farmer's daughters like the Cabyll-Ushtey or scare soldiers to death like Black Shuck, the English have, indeed, created a monster.

Ley Lines

The landscape of England is rich with traces of the past. A walk through the countryside will bring visitors to prehistoric burial mounds, imposing stone circles, picturesque medieval churches, and other monuments. At times it seems the land is stitched together by these relics, leaving many to wonder if somehow they're all connected.

Back in the 1920s, amateur archaeologist Alfred Watkins suggested just that. In two influential books, *Early British Trackways* and *The Old Straight Track*, he theorized that straight lines crisscross the English landscape, marked by prehistoric monuments and natural features such as hilltops and fords. These, he said, were England's first roads, giving prehistoric Britons easy access to natural resources. Watkins called these lines "ley lines", and he suggested they were part of the country's lost heritage stamped out by the conquering Romans.

Watkins

But not all the knowledge was lost. People continued to use the ley lines, and even those who didn't know their true purpose instinctively sensed their power. Thus, many later buildings of importance, especially medieval churches and holy wells, were built on ley lines. Watkins traced a large number of these lines on his tireless tramps through the countryside. With the help of

Ordnance Survey maps, an impressively detailed set of maps that shows all human and manmade features down to exacting detail, he was able to trace many leys. He encouraged his readers to try it for themselves. One didn't even have to leave the house; owning a ruler and a set of maps was the only requirement.

His ideas were met with derision by the archaeological community, and with justifiable reason. Watkins offered no proof, often ignored important ancient sites that weren't on his lines, and failed to adequately explain why prehistoric people would drive straight tracks through the landscape when, as every hiker knows, the easiest route from one point to another is almost always a meandering path through the most gentle terrain. Archaeologists also pointed out that the English countryside is filled with ancient sites, and with any dense scattering of points it's easy enough to connect a few in a straight line through random chance.

The public reaction, on the other hand, was the exact opposite. In the 1920s and '30s, England was going through a boom in outdoor activities. Local societies sponsored country walks specializing in history, geology, nature, birdwatching, and every other imaginable subject. A Mass Trespass movement organized crowds of hikers to go through farmers' fields in order to champion their cause of right of way through a open countryside, a cause they eventually won and that hikers still enjoy today. This "back to the land" movement coincided was a rise in interest in archaeology and the occult, two disparate fields that walked hand in hand down the ley lines.

Soon leys were springing up everywhere as individuals and dedicated groups tromped through the English countryside or sat at home by the fire, studying their sets of Ordnance Survey maps. Ley hunting became a sort of intellectual craze, a way to connect with one's own land and heritage.

After a time the craze faded as the English took on more serious matters such as World War II and the hard economic decade of the 1950s. But the idea of ley lines never entirely died. It took a new generation, with very different ideas, to bring them back into the limelight.

This was thanks in large part to paranormal writer John Michell, whose 1969 book *The View of Atlantis*, spun the antiquarian idea for the hippy generation. Basing his ideas on feng shui, the Chinese art of harmonizing with the universe and channeling energy through the placement of objects, he wrote that ley lines were lines of earth energy and that ancient peoples tapped into these currents by placing monuments such as stone circles upon them. In this view, lay lines were not specifically English, rather the English lines were part of a global network of ley lines powering the planet. Michell's book sold well and went through a number of printings and a later expanded edition.

Ley lines are still a major part of paranormal belief in England today. There are several societies dedicated to hunting leys, and they are still using Watkins' old techniques of field walking and map studying. There is a great deal of debate over the old and new interpretations of ley lines, with more scientifically minded ley hunters saying they were part of an ancient religion, while more New Age investigators say this religion is in fact the true one, and that ley lines are the key to living harmoniously with Mother Earth. Many of the latter group use dowsing in order to detect the Earth power running through the ley lines. The paranormal interest in ley lines would surprise if not disappoint Watkins; as John Bruno Hare noted, "Watkins never attributed any supernatural significance to leys; he believed that they were simply pathways that had been used for trade or ceremonial purposes, very ancient in origin, possibly dating back to the Neolithic, certainly pre-Roman. .. He was an intensely rational person with an active intellect, and I think he would be a bit disappointed with some of the fringe aspects of ley lines today."

While ley lines seem to be more the product of nostalgia and wishful thinking, walking a ley can be quite enjoyable even without believing in its existence. Many go through some of the most beautiful parts of the countryside the nation has to offer, passing ancient monuments steeped in folklore and history. For example, two leys called the Thornborough Leys in Yorkshire offer a fine hike, one that can be made along access routes through stretches of private property thanks to those Mass Trespassers of the 1930s.

One ley starts at the Thornborough Henges and heads southeast over 11 miles of open, rolling landscape. Henges are circular or oval-shaped earthen banks with an internal ditch that surrounds a central flat area. They were common in the Neolithic period although their use is disputed. The Thornborough Henges are a series of three henges, each about 780 feet in diameter with connecting avenues made by parallel earthen banks up to 16 feet high. The henges date to around 3500-2500 BCE, and the entire grouping is more than a mile long from the northwest to the southeast, the direction of the ley line. Archaeological excavation has revealed that the sides of the earthen banks were originally cover in gypsum, making it shine white in the sunlight. Archaeologists have also noted that the middle henge is slightly off from the line, imitating the pattern of stars in Orion's belt. Several Bronze Age burial mounds are scattered around the site.

The henges and mounds are built over the earlier Thornborough Cursus. A cursus is a large, cigar-shaped enclosure made by a ditch, generally with burials alongside it. Archaeologists say these strange enclosures were used for parades and rituals, but no one is really sure. The cursus actually runs northeast-southwest, and so doesn't align with the ley or the henges.

Tony Newbold's picture of the Thornborough henges

The ley line continues across fields and low hills to the Nunwick Henge, a lone henge that isn't very visible anymore thanks to being in the center of a centuries-old farmer's field. The ley ends at the Devil's Arrows, one of the most visually stunning collections of megaliths anywhere in England. They are three large menhirs (standing stones) dating to the late Neolothic or early Bronze Age, c. 2500 BC. The tallest stone measures 22 feet and 6 inches tall. They stand in a line and are of millstone grit that erodes with the rain to make strange grooved designs that give the stones a distinctive appearance. Archaeologists have discovered there were originally five stones – one fell down sometime in antiquity and another was pulled down in the 18th century by people hoping to find treasure underneath it.

The Devil's Arrows

The stones get their name from an old folktale about the Devil, who, angered at the town of Aldborough, threw stones at it while standing on nearby Howe Hill. The stones fell short, however, thanks to the piety of the people. There are many similar tales attached to standing stones across England.

Two other tales attached to the stones comes from the October 1860 edition of *The Geologist*. A correspondent who visited the stones and collected local stories about them wrote:

> "Their name, as the Devil's Arrows, seems to have originated from the following story, which we had related to us by an hoary headed individual living in Boroughbridge, when soliciting information as to their history:
>
> "There lived a very pious old man (a Druid should we imagine) who was reckoned an excellent cultivator of the soil. However, during each season at the

time his crops had come to maturity they were woefully pillaged by his surrounding neighbours; so that at this, he being provokingly grieved, the Devil appeared, telling the old man if he would only recant and throw away his holiness he should never more be disturbed in his mind, or have whatever he grew stolen or demolished.

"The old man, like Eve in the garden, yielded to temptation, and at once obeyed the impulse of Satan for the benefit of worldly gain. So when the old man's crops were again being pillaged, the Devil threw from the infernal regions some ponderous arrows, which so frightened the plunderers by shaking the earth that never more was he harrassed in that way. Hence the name of the 'Devil's Arrows.'

"Another individual told me that it was believed by some that the stones sprung up one night in the very places they now occupy. These opinions seem to be somewhat firmly fixed in the minds of the narrators. A superstition once imbibed is in many instances difficult to eradicate. However, we neither believe nor wish others to believe that they either sprung up in a single night, or were shot from a bow of Satan."

A second ley line starts by running along two of the Devil's Arrows and shoots across the Yorkshire landscape for five miles to the south-southeast. The route aligns with the Cana Henge, another henge that can only faintly be seen today, and ends up descending into the Ure Valley and ending at the Hutton Moor Henge. This last henge is a bit more visible on the ground and is impressive in size, measuring 680 feet in diameter and thus comparable to the Thornborough Henges.

Hutton Moor Henge was much better preserved 150 years ago, and it was described in detail by the antiquarian John Walbran in his 1851 book *A Guide to Ripon, Harrogate, Fountains Abbey, Bolton Priory*. While his interpretation of the site includes the now disproven idea that megalithic constructions were the handiwork of the Celtic Druids, it does give some details of the site that have since been lost:

"Though recent agricultural operations have partially effaced the regularity and proportion of its plan, it is sufficiently evident that it was enclosed by a lofty mound and corresponding trench—the latter being inside, and a platform or space about thirty feet wide intervening.

"…At two opposite points, bearing nearly north and south, the mound and trench, for about the space of twenty-five feet, have been discontinued, in order to form an approach to the area of the temple. Outside the mound, also, are some slight vestiges of a further avenue, but too indefinite to be traced. But, however obscure the denotation of its several parts may have become, the antiquity and purpose of the place, as a temple for the performance of Druidical rites, is satisfactorily ascertained by the existence of at least eight large Celtic barrows in its immediate vicinity; one of which, being on the very ridge of the vale, and planted with fir trees, forms a conspicuous and useful object to guide a stranger to the site. Two of these barrows were opened five years ago, but I found nothing but a few calcined human bones, the ashes of the oaken funeral pile, and some fragments of flint arrow-heads, such as are still used by the North-American Indians. Several bronze spear-heads and celts [axe heads] have, however, been found in the neighbourhood, within recollection.

"…two small pyramids or obelisks, [were] built on the mound of the temple, about fifty years ago, in the place, it is said, of two similar erections, apparently of high antiquity."

It is interesting to note that the ley line passes right through one of the barrows, or burial mounds, that Walbran mentions. It's also interesting to compare the entrances to the Hutton Moor Henge and the A1 highway less than a mile to the east. They are nearly parallel. The A1, it turns out, runs along the course of an old Roman road. In fact, all the henges of the Ure Valley have entrances that parallel nearby Roman roads. Why this should be the case is unclear. It's yet another of the many strange alignments found in the ancient English landscape.

Holy Wells

No coverage of British folk magic would be complete without mentioning the numerous sacred wells that imbue the landscape with so much of its character. Water has always had a central place in the spiritual life of the British Isles and Europe. As early as the Neolithic era, people were throwing offerings into bogs and other bodies of water, and some of these sacrifices have been preserved through time and discovered by archaeologists in modern times. Two of England's most famous Celtic artifacts, the celebrated horned helmet and enameled shield that adorn the covers of so many books on the Celts, were sacrificial offerings found in modern times in the River Thames.

The ancient Celtic "Waterloo Helmet" found in the Thames

The scared nature of water has survived in the magical landscape in the form of holy wells. Many of these wells date to prehistoric times, were co-opted by the Church at the dawn of Christianity, and have endured through the centuries as gathering places for worship and healing. During the 19th century revival of interest in folklore, several countrywide surveys were conducted and it was found that every county had dozens of such wells. They were most common in areas where the Celtic culture was better preserved, such as Cornwall, Wales, and Scotland.

In the 21st century, it is impossible to figure out their original purpose and meaning. Perhaps no one meaning ever existed. Certainly, in later times, their meanings and uses became fragmented and were reworked in each era to serve that era's needs.

During the initial spread of churches in the 5th century A.D., there was a determined effort to take over pagan sacred wells and give them Christian interpretations. One example can be found at the Church of St. Margaret's in Binsey, Oxfordshire. The church was founded in the late 7th century by St. Frideswide, the daughter of a Saxon Christian nobleman who moved to a pagan area and preached the Gospel. When a local pagan leader tried to seduce her, God struck him blind. Taking pity on him, she prayed to St. Margaret of Antioch and a holy well sprung out of the earth. The water cured the pagan's eyes, and soon St. Frideswide had many converts.

A church was built next to the holy well. Like many early Christian churches in Britain, it went through several phases of construction, but it still retains some of its Norman-era features. It became hugely popular as a pilgrimage site for people searching for cures, and the walls were covered with the crutches of pilgrims who arrived lame and left walking with confidence. The well even made it into one of the most popular children's books of all time when Lewis Carroll used it in *Alice's Adventure in Wonderland* as the "treacle well." "Treacle" is a medieval term for any "healing fluid."

In the mid-to-late 20th century, visitors to the well tapered off, and it became disused and partially forgotten. Then, in the early 21st century, it experienced a revival. People came to honor the stone-lined well, which stands just outside the church. A tree that overhangs the well is decorated with bells and ribbons and often candles and coins are left around its lip. In the last several years, the well's popularity has waned and waxed, but it has never died out.

Many British holy wells specialized in the ailments they cured, such as rickets, eye problems, and even leprosy. Some were said to help with women's fertility, such as one holy well at Willie's Muir in Scotland, where the most unchristian observances were held by the local village women, who "rolled up their skirts and petticoats till their wames [bellies] were bare. The auld wife gave them the sign to step around her and away they went, one after the other, wi' the sun, round the spring, each one holding up her coats like she was holding herself to the sun. As each one came anent her, the auld wife took up the water in her hands and threw it on their wames. Never a one cried out at the cold o' the water and never a word was spoken. Three times round they went. The auld wife made a sign to them. They dropped their coats to their feet again, synt [then] they opend their dress frae the neck and skipped it off their shoulders so that their paps [breasts] sprang out. The auld wife gave them another sign. They doun on their knees afore her, across the spring; and she took up the water in her hands, skirpit [splashed it] on their paps, three times three. Then the auld wife rose and the three barren women rose. The put on their claes again and drew their shawls about their faces and left the hollow without a word spoken and scattered across the muir for hame."

There was generally a ritual associated with the well in order to activate the cure. A common one was to arrive at the well with a rag tied around the afflicted area, which would then be hung on a nearby tree. With other wells it was necessary to soak the rag in the well, wipe the area, and then hang it on the tree. As the rag slowly rotted away, so would the disease slowly fade. At other wells, candles or pins would be left. The well of St. Agnes on the Scilly Isles off the coast of Cornwall was frequented by wreckers, a rather nasty type of criminal who would set up fake lighthouses on stormy nights in order to lure ships onto the rocks. The broken ships would then be looted and any survivors were killed. The wreckers were audacious enough to leave bent pins at the well along with a prayer in order to get the saint to send them a rich prize!

There were often specific days when people should come, at either an old Celtic festival such as Summer Solstice, or the saint's day of an associated saint. It was common for the people to arrive at dawn, approach from a particular direction, and circumambulate the well three times. This was the case at the well of St. Fillan in Perthshire, which cured madness. The unfortunate person had to be led three times around the pool, calling out first the name of the Father, then the name of the Son, and lastly the Holy Spirit. He was then immersed in the water in the name of the Holy Trinity.

Of all the types of folk magic in Britain, holy wells seem to be the most capable of surviving modern lack of interest. While witch bottles, magical texts, and curses have mostly disappeared, holy wells still have their devotees. Perhaps it is the association with modern Christian churches, or perhaps it is something deeper, related to the sacred nature of the landscape, but something in their nature has resonated with the era of the Internet and cell phones. In an age cut off from its roots and disassociated from the land, there are still thousands of people who make the journey to ancient holy wells to say a few prayers and make offerings. The magic of Britain still lives.

Charms and Spells

Like old shoes and dead cats, written charms have also been used by the English for centuries. Many of the papers perished over the centuries thanks to mice and dampness, but those that do survive give insight into the thoughts and fears of people from the time. Charms have been found stuck between stones in walls, placed in bottles, and dropped into wells and other secret hiding places.

This specialized magic would be practiced by a local cunning person, a person believed capable of rare magical powers. Like charms from all cultures, these short spells often took the form of prayers and included bits of Latin (often so badly misspelled as to be nearly illegible), Bible passages, and astrological and other magical symbols. For example, one charm from Powys, Wales reads in part, "Lord Jesus Christ be the preserver of William Pentrynant his cows, calves, milk, butter, cattle of all ages, mares, suckers, horses, of all ages yews, lambs, sheep of all ages, pigs, sows and prosper him on this farm to live luckily saved from all witchcraft and evil men or women spirits or wizards or hardness of heart amen."

As that charm suggests, it was typical for charms to call on the Father, Son, or Holy Ghost, or indeed, all three, for protection. While some researchers have tried to find links to pre-Christian practices or suggest a lingering paganism in folk magic, the fact is that whatever their origins, these spells became firmly rooted in Christian beliefs.

This can be seen in the curses as well. Perhaps the most famous curse in Britain is on the so-called Carlisle Cursing Stone, found on the border between England and Scotland. This stone is not ancient but was carved and installed in front of the regional museum in 2000. It does, however, contain an old curse, first laid down by the Archbishop of Glasgow, Gavin Dunbar, against the Border Reivers in 1525. The Reivers were Scottish bandits who raided across the border, stealing livestock and any other valuables from the English. Some Scots celebrated them, and still do, as national freedom fighters, but at the time, most people thought of them as simple criminals. Their incursions got so bad that the border was dotted with small private castles built by local nobility to protect their peasants and herds.

Archbishop Dunbar's curse runs:

> "I curse their head and all the hairs of their head; I curse their face, their brain [thoughts], their mouth, their nose, their tongue, their teeth, their forehead, their shoulders, their breast, their heart, their stomach, their back, their womb, their arms, their leggs, their hands, their feet, and every part of their body, from the top of their head to the soles of their feet, before and behind, within and without.

> "I curse them going and I curse them riding; I curse them standing and I curse them sitting; I curse them eating and I curse them drinking; I curse them rising, and I curse them lying; I curse them at home, I curse them away from home; I curse them within the house, I curse them outside of the house; I curse their wives, their children, and their servants who participate in their deeds. I [bring ill wishes upon] their crops, their cattle, their wool, their sheep, their horses, their swine, their geese, their hens, and all their livestock. I [bring ill wishes upon] their halls, their chambers, their kitchens, their stanchions, their barns, their cowsheds, their barnyards, their cabbage patches, their plows, their harrows, and the goods and houses that are necessary for their sustenance and welfare.

> "May all the malevolent wishes and curses ever known, since the beginning of the world, to this hour, light on them. May the malediction of God, that fell upon Lucifer and all his fellows, that cast them from the high Heaven to the deep hell, light upon them.

> "May the fire and the sword that stopped Adam from the gates of Paradise, stop them from the glory of Heaven, until they forebear, and make amends.

> "May the evil that fell upon cursed Cain, when he slew his brother Abel, needlessly, fall on them for the needless slaughter that they commit daily.

> "May the malediction that fell upon all the world, man and beast, and all that ever took life, when all were drowned by the flood of Noah, except Noah and his ark, fall upon them and drown them, man and beast, and make this realm free of them, for their wicked sins.

> "May the thunder and lightning which rained down upon Sodom and Gomorra and all the lands surrounding them, and burned them for their vile sins, rain down upon them and burn them for their open sins. May the evil and confusion that fell

on the Gigantis for their oppression and pride in building the Tower of Babylon, confound them and all their works, for their open callous disregard and oppression.

"May all the plagues that fell upon Pharoah and his people of Egypt, their lands, crops and cattle, fall upon them, their equipment, their places, their lands, their crops and livestock.

"May the waters of the Tweed and other waters which they use, drown them, as the Red Sea drowned King Pharoah and the people of Egypt, preserving God's people of Israel.

"May the earth open, split and cleave, and swallow them straight to hell, as it swallowed cursed Dathan and Abiron, who disobeyed Moses and the command of God.

"May the wild fire that reduced Thore and his followers to two-hundred-fifty in number, and others from 14,000 to 7,000 at anys, usurping against Moses and Aaron, servants of God, suddenly burn and consume them daily, for opposing the commands of God and Holy Church.

"May the malediction that suddenly fell upon fair Absolom, riding through the wood against his father, King David, when the branches of a tree knocked him from his horse and hanged him by the hair, fall upon these untrue Scotsmen and hang them the same way, that all the world may see.

"May the malediction that fell upon Nebuchadnezzar's lieutenant, Olifernus, making war and savagery upon true christian men; the malediction that fell upon Judas, Pilate, Herod, and the Jews that crucified Our Lord; and all the plagues and troubles that fell on the city of Jerusalem therefore, and upon Simon Magus for his treachery, bloody Nero, Ditius Magcensius, Olibrius, Julianus Apostita and the rest of the cruel tyrants who slew and murdered Christ's holy servants, fall upon them for their cruel tyranny and murder of Christian people.

"And may all the vengeance that ever was taken since the world began, for open sins, and all the plagues and pestilence that ever fell on man or beast, fall on them for their openly evil ways, senseless slaughter and shedding of innocent blood.

"I sever and part them from the church of God, and deliver them immediately to the devil of hell, as the Apostle Paul delivered Corinth. I bar the entrance of all places they come to, for divine service and ministration of the sacraments of holy church, except the sacrament of infant baptism, only; and I forbid all churchmen to hear their confession or to absolve them of their sins, until they are first humbled/subjugated by this curse.

"I forbid all christian men or women to have any company with them, eating, drinking, speaking, praying, lying, going, standing, or in any other deed-doing, under the pain of deadly sin.

"I discharge all bonds, acts, contracts, oaths, made to them by any persons, out of loyalty, kindness, or personal duty, so long as they sustain this cursing, by which no man will be bound to them, and this will be binding on all men.

"I take from them, and cast down all the good deeds that ever they did, or shall do, until they rise from this cursing.

"I declare them excluded from all matins, masses, evening prayers, funerals or other prayers, on book or bead (rosary); of all pigrimages and alms deeds done, or to be done in holy church or be christian people, while this curse is in effect.

"And, finally, I condemn them perpetually to the deep pit of hell, there to remain with Lucifer and all his fellows, and their bodies to the gallows of Burrow moor, first to be hanged, then ripped and torn by dogs, swine, and other wild beasts, abominable to all the world. And their candle (light of their life) goes from your sight, as may their souls go from the face of God, and their good reputation from the world, until they forebear their open sins, aforesaid, and rise from this terrible cursing and make satisfaction and penance."

It's quite a litany, and it still has the power to intimidate today, despite its numerous spelling errors. When the Cursing Stone was erected in Carlisle as part of the Millennium celebrations in 2001, a local Christian group protested, saying that it showed their religion in a poor light. Others missed the fact that it was a Christian curse at all, and complained that public funds had been used to erect a monument dedicated to black magic! Perhaps in conjunction with that, others claim the stone has laid a curse on the local area. The same year it was erected, foot-and-mouth disease devastated livestock in the area, financially ruining many farmers. There was also a serious flood, but what was perhaps even worse was that Carlisle United Football Team got relegated. Local councilor Jim Tootle tried to get the stone removed, but he was met with derision from the less superstitious members of the Carlisle government. One of the reasons given for not removing the stone was, ironically enough, that the thousands of pounds needed to haul it away were needed for flood relief.

The artist who designed the stone, Gordon Young, angrily criticized locals who wanted to smash the stone, saying that he never intended it to be a monument to the occult, and that if he thought it was hurting Carlisle United's playing, he would smash it himself. Ironically, Young is a descendant of one of the Reiver families at which the curse was directed.

Some curses weren't so wordy. One curse from the late 19th century required the caster to burn salt on his fire at midnight and repeat a common cursing rhyme:

"This is not the thing I wish to burn

But Mrs. ____'s heart of _____ Somerset to turn

Wishing thee neither to eat, drink, sleep nor rest

Until thou dost come to me and do my request

Or else the wrath of God may fall on thee

And cause thee to be consumed in a moment – Amen."

Then the caster had to walk upstairs backwards while reciting the Lord's Prayer backwards, and remain silent until they went to bed.

One written charm found above the front door of a house in Lancashire said, "Sun, Moon, Mars, Jupiter, Venus, Saturn, Trine, Sextile, Dragon's Head, Dragon's Tail, I charge you all to gard this hause from all evils spirits whatever, and gard is from all Desorders, and from aney thing being taken wrangasly, and give this famaly good Ealth and Welth."

Other charms included old Catholic prayers in Latin, which had fallen out of official favor after Henry VIII's break with Rome. In one case from Suffolk in 1597, Margaret Neale was charged with witchcraft because she "taketh upon her to cure diseases by prayer, and therefore hath recourse of people to her farre and nighe. She confesses that she useth a prayer to God, and then the paternoster the creed and an other prayer devised, and before theis she useth to washe." She was found guilty of witchcraft and forced to stand in church with a sign hanging from her stating her crime. Considering how many witches were given the ultimate penalty for their crimes, perhaps the fact that Neale used prayers for her enchantments moved the judge to give her a more lenient sentence.

Written charms were common for all sorts of magic, likely because in an illiterate society, written words had power. Certain incantations appear again and again, like the old magical word "abracadabra." This word is first seen in the *Liber Medicinalis*, a Roman medical text dating to the 3rd century AD, but historians believe it is much older than that. Often, abracadabra was written out several times, with a letter taken off on each line. This created a triangle of letters:

```
A - B - R - A - C - A - D - A - B - R - A
A - B - R - A - C - A - D - A - B - R
A - B - R - A - C - A - D - A - B
A - B - R - A - C - A - D - A
```

```
A - B - R - A - C - A - D
  A - B - R - A - C - A
    A - B - R - A - C
      A - B - R - A
        A - B - R
          A - B
            A
```

The triangle, of course, is an old magical symbol. A charm with an abracadabra triangle was worn around the neck to ward away fever, evil spirits, and witches. It was often made of metal and worn as a necklace, handed down through the generations as a valuable item. Interestingly, the abracadabra triangle also appears in the *Liber Medicinalis*, a Roman charm that has lasted until the modern day.

Another charm to stave off fever comes from Lincolnshire:

"Father, Son and Holy Ghost,

Nail the Devil to a post,

Thrice I strike with holy crook,

One for God, one for Wod and one for Lok."

It's interesting that a couple of pagan gods, Woden (Odin) and Loki, made it into this otherwise Christian charm.

Some charms enjoyed widespread popularity and were used across Europe in various languages over the course of centuries. One example is a charm against sprains which begins with Christ's accident while riding.

"Our Lord forth raide,

His foal's foot slade:

Our Lord down lighted,

His foal's foot righted;

Saying: Flesh to flesh, blood to blood, and bane to bane,

In our Lord his name."

This charm was first recorded as being used by a cunning woman in the Orkney Islands, off the north coast of Scotland, in 1616. It was said at the time to be of great antiquity, and it continued to be popular for centuries thereafter. This spell was popular for curing sprains, and while it seems no more efficacious to modern minds than any of the other charms, it endured. One suspects that the sprain was treated with more mundane techniques as well, but that the charm gave the patient an extra bit of confidence.

Hummadruz

Another oddity of the English landscape, and one that is more verifiable, is the so-called "hummadruz." It's a strange word for a strange phenomenon. It refers to certain spots in the landscape where people will hear an unidentifiable buzz. It's usually a low humming or buzzing most often described as sounding like a large number of insects.

The term seems to have been coined in the 19th century and has a rather obscure origin. A good description of the hummadruz comes from the famous naturalist Gilbert White, who wrote in 1769, "There is a natural occurrence to be met with upon the highest part of our downs in hot summer days…a loud humming as of bees in the air, though not one insect is to be seen. The sound is distinctly to be heard the whole common through. Any person would suppose that a large swarm of bees was in motion and playing about his head."

White

Most people who experience one have been able to find the source for the sound, and all say that it's quite loud and distinct. Usually everyone in a group will hear it, but there are reports of only one person noticing the sound or that one person will hear it more loudly than the rest. Hummadruz can happen on hills or fields or by water, generally in remote areas and almost always on hot days.

The Earth Mysteries magazine *Northern Earth*, an excellent source for English oddities, has published numerous articles and letters about the sound. In issue 72 of that magazine, a reader who had heard it said that he and his wife used to keep bees and that the sound "was very like a contented hive, but there were no bees nearby."

Researchers have put forth various explanations, including Low-Frequency Noise sensitivity, electromagnetic sources, or atmospheric anomalies, but no single explanation really fits all cases. Technological explanations fall down in the face of historic descriptions such as Gilbert White's and the fact that most eyewitnesses report it in rural areas. Medical explanations such as tinnitus, a disorder within the ear that causes the patient to hear buzzing or ringing, doesn't explain why groups of people will hear the hummadruz or why it is specific to a location.

Another explanation is that it is some sort of earth energy along ley lines or spiritual locations. Paranormal investigators point out that many of the reports occur near historic spots such as holy wells or stone circles. While an appealing interpretation for some, there has been no statistical study to back this up, not to mention the fact that most people hiking in the countryside are attracted to these historic places, which may have been the point of the walk in the first place.

The hummadruz most likely has a natural explanation, one that scientists haven't bothered to investigate yet. A similar strange sound has been tracked down to its source. In many ports around the world, residents report a loud hum starting at night and going on for several hours. Hythe in Southampton was one such port. The mystery sound started in the autumn of 2013; every night at around 10:00 p.m., a loud hum would start up that would last all night. It got so bad that some residents moved in with friends in other towns in order to get some sleep. Scientists suggested that it could be the mating call of the midshipman fish (*Porichthys notatus*). The males of the species, while only measuring six inches, let out a loud hum when searching for a mate. If enough midshipmen fish are congregated in an area, the sound can be amplified by resonating off of ship's hulls and buildings. Midshipmen fish were found to be the culprits in a recurrent hum at ports in California and Seattle.

Since so many reports of the hummadruz occur well away from water, amorous fish cannot be used as an explanation.

English Ghosts

England is, of course, famous for its ghosts. Given the thousands of old houses, castles, churches, and battlefields in this land, it could be no other way.

Even its most famous buildings are allegedly haunted. Hampton Court Palace, home to 500 years of royalty, is said to have several ghosts. The most famous is Catherine Howard, the fifth wife of Henry VIII.

Catherine was still a teenager when she married an obese and, some say, impotent king. It wasn't long before Henry accused her of having an affair with the courtier Thomas Culpeper and put her under house arrest. The two had flirted before her marriage to the king, so these accusations may have been true or may have been the result of an increasingly moody and jealous monarch. She was confined to her quarters, but one day she managed to break free from her guards and ran down one of the palace hallways towards a room where Henry was praying, hoping to beg for her life. Before she could see the king, the guards grabbed her and dragged her back to her quarters as she screamed and struggled. She was later beheaded in the Tower of London. According to rumor, her last words were, "I die a Queen, but I would rather have died the wife of Culpeper." Centuries later, in this same hallway, generations of visitors and palace staff have heard screams at all hours of the day and night as the teenage queen's terror supposedly echoes down the centuries. For more than a hundred years it has been known as the Haunted Gallery.

Catherine Howard

Another of Henry's wives, who managed to die of natural causes, Jane Seymour, is also said to haunt the palace. In 1537 she gave birth to Henry's first son after years of disappointment and two previous wives not providing him with an heir. The future King Edward VI was born healthy, but his mother suffered complications from the delivery and died shortly after giving birth. A distraught Henry wrote to the king of France, "Divine Providence…hath mingled my joy with bitterness of the death of her who brought me this happiness."

Jane Seymour

The room where she died is at the top of the Silver Stick Stairs, named after the sign of office of one of the king's attendants. Every year around the anniversary of Seymour's death, a ghostly apparition of a woman dressed all in white is seen passing down the stairs holding a candle, heading for the rooms where her infant had his nursery.

The palace seems to be getting new ghosts as well. One, dubbed by the press as "Skeletor", made his appearance as recently as 2003. For three consecutive days, a CCTV camera caught a set of fire doors flying violently open. On the first day there was no apparent cause. On the second day they burst open, a strange, elongated male figure in what appeared to be Tudor era dress passed into the doorway from the inside and then closed the doors. The next day the doors again flew open, but this time Skeletor did not make an appearance. What's interesting is that when the doors burst open on the second day, Skeletor wasn't behind them; the doors, like on the other days, opened all by themselves. The purported ghost only closed them. The palace as CCTV cameras in countless locations and the figure wasn't seen approaching or leaving the area. He came out of nowhere, and vanished just as abruptly.

In London, another popular tourist attraction is the British Museum. Although visitors flock there to see its Egyptian mummies, there's a very English mummy not far off in University College on Gower Street. One of the cofounders of the college was Jeremy Bentham (1748-1832), who felt that Christian burial was a pointless waste and that corpses should be used for scientific investigation and then preserved as a monument. True to his word, he left orders in his will to be publicly dissected and then mummified. His dissection was performed during a fierce thunderstorm that some traditionalists interpreted as the wrath of God. Nevertheless it was well attended by his friends.

Bentham

However, his mummification did not go so well. The doctors tried to imitate a Maori recipe for mummification but the head turned out a hideous mess, with blackened, leathery skin that did not resemble the jowly Englishman in the least. So the doctors cut off his head and replaced it with a wax model topped with Bentham's own hair. The body was then dressed in his clothes, complete with his favorite walking stick and seated in an "auto-icon", a glass-fronted cabinet in the university. His head was placed to his side but later put under lock and key when some students were caught playing football with it.

At times, students whisper, Bentham leaves his case and can be seen walking down the hall. Sometimes he's not seen, but the rhythmic tapping of his walking stick signals that his spirit is on the move. Perhaps it is restless, and Bentham should have opted for a more traditional burial.

Bentham isn't the only Englishman to be strangely preserved after his death. A few centuries before, the Lord Lovell came to an untimely end and is believed to have turned into a ghost. Lord Lovell was born around 1455 or 1456 to a noble but not particularly important family. His father died when he was only 9, and he became a ward of King Edward IV, who gave him to Richard Neville, Earl of Warwick, to rear and educate. In the same household was the king's nine-year-old brother Richard. The two boys became best friends, and grew up learning the knightly arts of fighting, etiquette, dance, and music.

Edward IV

When Richard grew into manhood, he didn't forget his childhood friend, and he subsequently raised him to high station. Richard became King Richard III in 1483, and Lord Lovell became his right-hand man. He proved his loyalty by fighting alongside him against the rival for the throne, Henry VII, at the Battle of Bosworth Field in 1485, the turning point in the War of the Roses. Richard was killed and Lovell was forced to flee.

Richard III

Lovell's loyalty lasted beyond his friend's death, as he led a rebellion against the new king, only to be defeated at the Battle of Stoke in 1487. Once again Lovell was on the run and this time he fled to his country retreat at Minster Lovell Hall near Oxford. Fearing that his servants might betray him, he hid himself in a secret room in the cellar that was unknown to them. And there he stayed, never to leave.

It's unclear what happened, but historians surmise that he couldn't open the door and his desperate pleas for aid went unheard. What is known is that workmen discovered the secret chamber in 1718, breaking through and finding the skeleton of a man seated at a table, its withered hand resting on some papers. Did these papers contain the last words of Lord Lovell? It will never be known, because the air rushing in from the breach in the room soon turned what remained of the Lord Lovell, and his papers, to dust.

Many English people believe the ruins of Minster Lovell Hall on the banks of the River Windrush are still haunted by the unfortunate lord today. He can be seen at night, wandering through gutted doors and past the crumbling walls, still trying to summon a servant to release him from his self-imposed prison.

While people tend to think of hauntings being attached to specific places, preferably old ruins or dank and forbidding mansions, even everyday objects can be haunted. The English seem to have a fondness for haunted beds, and the most famous is the Great Bed of Ware. "Great" in this context means "large", and that it certainly is. This giant oak four-poster measures 11'1" long and 10'8.5" wide. It was constructed in the 15th century by Jonas Fosbrooke for King Edward IV. After the murder of the king's son, the bed was given away and was used by various inns in Ware through the years, especially during festival days when there was a shortage of beds. It was not uncommon in those days for people to share beds in an inn, and four or five could lie in the Great Bed of Ware quite comfortably.

Fosbrooke, who had been proud of his work for the king, resented that common folk were now using his masterpiece and decided to get even. Being dead didn't stop him. He began to haunt the bed, pinching and scratching its occupants. Bedbugs were apparently ruled out as the culprits. Fosbrooke was so picky that when Harrison Saxby, Henry VIII's Master of Horse, dared to sleep in the Great Bed of Ware in order to impress a lovely local lass, Fosbrooke gave him such a series of spectral wallops that by morning he was covered in bruises. Not even a trusted royal attendant could use the bed, though Saxby did win the girl's heart. For many years the bed was exhibited in the Crown Inn at Ware, and visitors would nightly toast it and its ghost.

The Tower of London is considered perhaps the most haunted of any building in the city. The Tower of London is one of the most historic sites in all of England, and still one of the most popular. All around is the modern City of London, one of the world's most prosperous and power financial districts, but the Tower is still a daunting structure that looms across the landscape. Not a single structure but a vast network of medieval and early modern fortifications, it anchors the southeastern end of the old City and controls access to the River Thames and, through it, London's connection to the sea. While the both the City and the Thames are often obscured by the walls once visitors are inside the Tower, they are inextricably tied to the building, giving the Tower its entire reason for existence.

Even today, taking a tour of the Tower can seemingly bring its history to life. Inside the visitor center are replicas of a crown, an executioner's axe and similar artifacts, but for most visitors, this is just the start. After they cross a small courtyard and approach the first gate, known as the

Middle Tower, they come to a stone bridge over a now-dry moat and enter the castle itself through the Byward Tower. The Tower, like many fortresses of its day, was built in concentric rings, so inside the outer wall is a narrow strip of land before the inner walls. Long, narrow buildings line the inside of the outer wall, and to the left along Mint Street these structures once housed the operation of the Royal Mint, making all of the coins of the realm.

From there, most visitors continue straight along, typically guided by one of the colorfully-dressed Yeoman Guards (the famous "Beefeaters"). Under the watch of the Bell Tower, they continue along the south face of the inner wall, on Water Lane, and just ahead is the famed Traitor's Gate; while today the area around here is paved and dry, in earlier times this was a "watergate" that allowed boats entry to the fortress. It was so named because this was the entrance by which prisoners (often traitors) entered the fortress, often never to leave. Ahead is Wakefield Tower, the entrance to the inner courtyards and a space that can be rented for small banquets and private dinners.

Inside the inner courtyards, visitors get a good first look at the White Tower, the 11th century Norman castle at the heart of the Tower (and the original "Tower" the entire complex is named for). Built of distinctive white stone, it has been a beacon of royal power for centuries. It is four stories tall and at points has walls of up to 15 feet thick, with towers on the four corners that have cupolas atop them (added much later than the original structure). Within the Tower is an impressive collection of medieval armor and arms, as well as the well-preserved St. John's Chapel. Directly behind the White Tower is the Waterloo Block, also known as the Jewel House. A perennial favorite of visitors, the Crown Jewels of the United Kingdom are stored here when not in use.

In the southeast corner of the inner courtyard (the "Inner Ward") is a charming green space backed by lovely Tudor structures whose calm belies their bloody history. This is the Tower Green, which was the location of the executions of all of those prisoners who were given "Private" deaths (as opposed to a "Public" death which occurred outside the walls on Tower Hill before the London mob). It is perhaps best known as the site of the deaths of three of Henry VIII's wives: Anne Boleyn, Catherine Howard, and Jane Grey. One of the surrounding buildings, the Queen's House, was named after its most famous prisoner - Anne Boleyn - but was also the site of the trial of the notorious Guy Fawkes.

Anne Boleyn

Other sites within the walls of the Tower include the famous ravens (according to legend, if they ever leave the Tower the monarchy will fall), the museum of the Royal Regiment of Fusiliers (whose ceremonial commander is the Constable of the Tower) and the Ceremony of the Keys. The Ceremony is performed nightly by the Yeoman Warders when they seal the gates of the Tower and the Chief Warder passes the keys to the Resident Governor. Just beyond the Tower rises the great supports of the Tower Bridge (often confused with the smaller London Bridge) and the Thames.

Ultimately, it's impossible to fully appreciate the Tower without understanding its context. Like all fortresses, it was built to control and protect its surroundings, and the history of the Tower is bound up in the mutual histories of London and the Monarchy. The unfolding saga of war, imprisonment, glory, and treason in England can all be told through the lens of the Tower, and the lives that intersected with it.

Set on an old Celtic sacred hill and a later Roman fort, the famous White Tower, the main building still standing, was built by William the Conqueror in the 1070s to consolidate Norman control over the land. It has remained a symbol of royal rule ever since, and for many centuries served as a prison and place of execution for traitors. Thus, it comes as no surprise that many believe restless phantoms supposedly haunt its grounds.

Bob Collowân's picture of the Tower of London

One account comes from no less a personage than Edmund Lenthal Swifte, who in the early 19th century served as Keeper of the Crown Jewels. In *Notes and Queries* for 1860, Swifte wrote of a strange occurrence that happened to him at the Tower:

> "I have often purposed to leave behind me a faithful record of all that I personally know of this strange story. Forty-three years have passed, and its impression is as vividly before me as on the moment of its occurrence…but there are yet survivors who can testify that I have not at any time either amplified or abridged my ghostly experiences.
>
> "In 1814 I was appointed Keeper of the Crown Jewels in the Tower, where I resided with my family till my retirement in 1852. One Saturday night in October, 1817, about 'the witching hour' I was at supper with my wife, her sister, and our little boy, in the sitting-room of the Jewel House, which then comparatively modernized is said to have been the 'doleful prison' of Anne Boleyn, and of the ten bishops whom Oliver Cromwell piously accommodated therein.

"The room was as it still is irregularly shaped, having three doors and two windows, which last are cut nearly nine feet deep into the outer wall; between these is a chimney-piece, projecting far into the room, and (then) surmounted with a large oil-painting. On the night in question the doors were all closed, heavy and dark cloth curtains were let down over the windows, and the only light in the room was that of two candles on the table; I sate at the foot of the table, my son on my right hand, his mother fronting the chimney-piece, and her sister on the opposite side. I had offered a glass of wine and water to my wife, when, on putting it to her lips, she paused, and exclaimed, 'Good God! What is that?' I looked up, and saw a cylindrical figure, like a glass-tube, seemingly about the thickness of my arm, and hovering between the ceiling and the table; its contents appeared to be a dense fluid, white and pale azure, like to the gathering of a summer-cloud, and incessantly mingling within the cylinder This lasted about two minutes, when it began slowly to move before my sister-in-law; then, following the oblong shape of the table, before my son and myself; passing behind my wife, it paused for a moment over her right shoulder [observe, there was no mirror opposite to her in which she could there behold it]. Instantly she crouched down, and with both hands covering her shoulder, she shrieked out, 'O Christ! It has seized me!' Even now, while writing, I feel the fresh horror of that moment. I caught up my chair, struck at the wainscot behind her, rushed upstairs to the other children's room, and told the terrified nurse what I had seen. Meanwhile, the other domestics had hurried into the parlour, where their mistress recounted to them the scene, even as I was detailing it above stairs.

"The marvel of all this is enhanced by the fact that neither my sister-in-law nor my son beheld this 'appearance.' When I the next morning related the night's horror to our chaplain, after the service in the Tower church, he asked me, might not one person have his natural senses deceived? And if one, why might not two? My answer was, if two, why not two thousand? An argument which would reduce history, secular or sacred, to a fable.

"Our chaplain suggested the possibilities of some foolery having been intromitted at my windows, and proposed the visit of a scientific friend, who minutely inspected the parlour, and made the closest investigation, but could not in any way solve the mystery."

That wasn't the only tale Swifte had to tell. He also spoke of a strange apparition witnessed by a guard: "One of the night-sentries at the Jewel Office was alarmed by a figure like a huge bear issuing from underneath the jewel-room door. He thrust at it with his bayonet, which stuck in the door, even as my chair dinted the wainscot; he dropped in a fit, and was carried senseless to the guard room. When on the morrow I saw the unfortunate soldier in the main guard room, his fellow-sentinel was also there, and testified to having seen him on his post just before the alarm, awake and alert, and even spoken to him. Moreover, I then heard the poor man tell his own story. I saw him once again on the following day, but changed beyond my recognition; in another day or two the brave and steady soldier, who would have mounted a breach or led a forlorn hope with unshaken nerves, died at the presence of a shadow."

Another of London's landmarks carries a baleful mystery. In the Egyptian gallery of the British Museum lies what has become known in popular folklore as "The Unlucky Mummy." More accurately, it is a mummy board, an inner coffin made of painted wood and plaster set directly over the mummy. One or two larger coffins would go outside the mummy board, and the whole affair would be placed in a stone sarcophagus. The mummy board is in the shape of a woman with crossed arms. It is elaborately painted and of such high quality that, although the identity of the occupant remains unknown, for many years it was assumed to belong to a member of royalty or a high priestess.

An early 20th century depiction of the Unlucky Mummy

The Unlucky Mummy was said to have been discovered by Egyptologist Thomas Douglas Murray and two friends while traveling in Egypt in 1889. While in Thebes, they were shown the fine mummy board by a mysterious Arab who was vague about where and when it was dug up. The three of them were so impressed by the artifact that they all wanted to buy it. To decide who would get the prize, they drew straws. Murray won - or lost, as later events would reveal.

After securing the prize, Murray packed up the mummy board, shipped it off to London, and sailed up the Nile to go hunting. Just a few days after sending his purchase away, he shot at some game on the banks of the Nile and the gun exploded in his hands. One arm was seriously injured, and he immediately ordered his boatman to return to Cairo so he could seek medical attention. A strong wind blew against the sails, and it took 10 days to reach their destination as the boatman struggled to move the craft down the river. By then Murray's arm had become infected, and a doctor in Cairo was forced to amputate.

While convalescing on the boat ride back to England, Murray was further shocked when one of his friends who had wanted to buy the mummy suddenly died. Three servants who had handled the mummy board also died within a few months.

Back in London, Murray unpacked the mummy board and put it on display for his many visitors. One prominent figure who came to see it was Madame H.P. Blavatsky, a clairvoyant and founder of the Theosophy movement. Blavatsky sensed an evil influence surrounding the artifact and urged Murray to get rid of it. Murray ignored this advice and lent it to several friends and acquaintances to display in their homes. This caused a string of ill luck, and soon no one wanted to take the mummy board. Some people died unexpectedly. Some people heard strange noises at night. In one house, all the glass in the room where the artifact sat on display suddenly shattered. One woman who photographed the mummy board was terrified when she developed the prints. Instead of a calm painted visage, staring out at her from the photograph was a living Egyptian woman with a furious and threatening expression. The photographer died within weeks of taking the image.

Blavatsky

At this point, Murray gave in and donated the mummy board to the British Museum. The workman who carted it from Murray's house to the museum died shortly thereafter.

The trouble continued at the museum. Night watchmen reported hearing sobs coming from inside the mummy case, and what sounded like someone pounding on the inside trying to get out. The museum staff tried to placate the spirit by giving it a prominent display and a sign praising the beauty of the artwork, but that mollified the restless spirit only a little. For years afterward, workers passing through the darkened Egyptian gallery at night would feel a sense of dread when they looked at the mummy case.

The oddest chapter of the story of the Unlucky Mummy concerns noted journalist W.T. Stead, who was the first to report on the curse of the mummy case. More sober minds might accuse him of making the whole thing up. What is certainly true, however, is that he and Murray asked museum officials for permission to hold a séance in the Egyptian Gallery to find out the reason behind the hauntings. The curators turned them down.

Then in 1912, Stead booked passage on a brand new ocean liner, both to enjoy the trip across the Atlantic and to cover the story of the inaugural voyage world's biggest ship—the *Titanic*. As the ship sank, he helped women and children into the lifeboats and then stayed behind after giving up the last place. He was never seen again.

The story soon circulated that the British Museum had sold the cursed mummy case to an American museum and that it was on board. The mummy's curse had led to the world's most famous nautical disaster!

Or not. In fact, the mummy case had never left the Egyptian gallery.

Ironically, the British Museum's online artifact catalog lists the mummy case as "The Unlucky Mummy," although it quickly goes on to pooh-pooh the story without giving any other explanation for its discovery or why it has attracted so many dire rumors. More prosaically, the website describes the mummy board as having Museum Number EA22542 and dating to the 21st Dynasty (c. 950 BC). It can be found in gallery 62, display case 21.

Spring-heeled Jack

One of the most bizarre creatures to be seen in England was Spring-heeled Jack, who terrorized London and the English countryside in the 19th century. He was first sighted in London in September of 1837. Lone pedestrians walking late at night would be startled by a freakish figure who would leap over tall fences and land in their path. Descriptions varied, as descriptions of crimes generally do, but most agreed that the figure looked like a devil. While the size and shape of a man, he had pointed ears, eyes that "resembled red balls of fire", and a black cloak. Some reported he wore a helmet and beneath his cloak he had a strange, tight fitting suit that looked like white oilskin. His fingertips were fitted with long metal claws. Some even said that he breathed blue flames from his mouth.

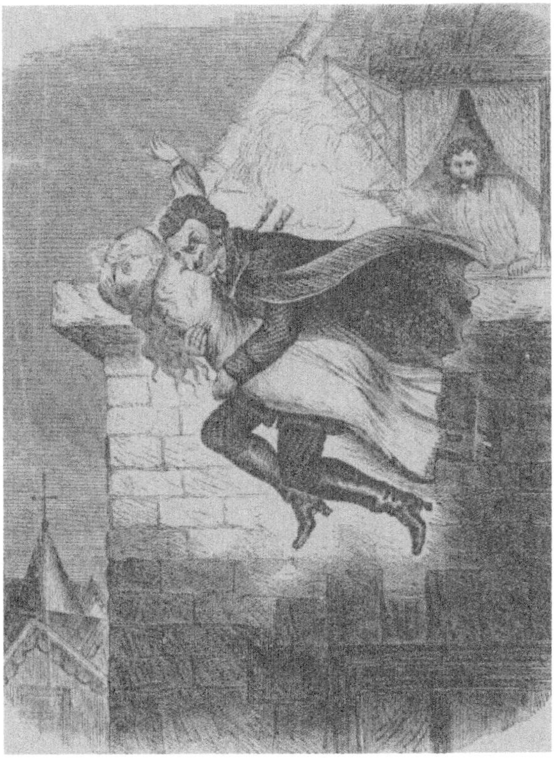

19th century depictions of Spring-Heeled Jack

An early 20th century depiction of Spring-heeled Jack

In October of that year, a servant girl names Mary Stevens was walking at night through Clapham Common when Spring-heeled Jack leapt out of an alley at her. He clutched her to him, kissing her as he raked at her clothes with his claws. The terrified girl said that his fingers felt "cold and clammy as those of a corpse." When she screamed, her attacker fled.

The next day, Spring-heeled Jack leapt in front of a carriage hurrying along a London road at night. The driver swerved and crashed, seriously injuring himself. As passersby ran to the scene, Spring-Heeled Jack leapt over a nine-foot wall to make his escape, laughing at his pursuers with a weird, high-pitched voice.

So many reports were coming in that on January 9, 1838, the Lord Mayor of London, Sir John Cowan, spoke of the mystery in a public speech. He read out an anonymous letter that he had received a few days earlier. The letter writer, who signed himself as "a resident of Peckham," asserted:

"It appears that some individuals (of, as the writer believes, the highest ranks of life) have laid a wager with a mischievous and foolhardy companion, that he durst not take upon himself the task of visiting many of the villages near London in three different disguises—a ghost, a bear, and a devil; and moreover, that he will not enter a gentleman's gardens for the purpose of alarming the inmates of the house. The wager has, however, been accepted, and the unmanly villain has succeeded in depriving seven ladies of their senses, two of whom are not likely to recover, but to become burdens to their families.

"At one house the man rang the bell, and on the servant coming to open door, this worse than brute stood in no less dreadful figure than a spectre clad most perfectly. The consequence was that the poor girl immediately swooned, and has never from that moment been in her senses.

"The affair has now been going on for some time, and, strange to say, the papers are still silent on the subject. The writer has reason to believe that they have the whole history at their finger-ends but, through interested motives, are induced to remain silent."

The mayor told the assembled crowd that he had received reports from boroughs all around the city and that many people, especially servant girls, the kind of women who would have to walk alone at night, had been injured by the mysterious attacker's claws. People in the crowd even claimed that some victims had died.

The mayor stated that some reports of Spring-heeled Jack's leaping abilities and breathing fire were "the greatest exaggerations," and that he did not believe "that the ghost performs the feats of a devil upon earth." On the contrary, he thought that it was some prankster, and that the guilty party would soon be brought to justice.

The next day, the *Morning Herald* discussed several sightings and noted that one of their reporters had "visited many of the places above mentioned, where he found that, although the stories were in everyone's mouth, no person who had actually seen the ghost could be found. He was directed to many persons who were named as having been injured by this alleged ghost, but, on his speaking to them, they immediately denied all knowledge of it, but directed him to other persons whom they had heard had been ill-treated, but with them he met with no better success, and the police…declare that, although they have made every enquiry into the matter, they cannot find one individual hardy enough to assert a personal knowledge on the subject."

This makes the whole affair sound like an urban legend, but the plot soon thickened, because so many reports were coming in that it was hard to dismiss them all. It's notable that many victims insisted it was a man in a costume, which makes it distinct from reports of ghosts or fairies that were common at the time. How this man could breath fire and make leaps that would break a normal person's ankles is another question.

Another frightening attack occurred on the night of February 19, 1838. According to press reports, a young woman named Jane Alsop heard a loud knock on her door and the cry, "I'm a police officer. For God's sake, bring me a light, for we have caught Spring-heeled Jack in the lane!" Fetching a candle and opening the door, she saw a dark, cloaked figure. She handed him the candle and then he threw back his cloak and revealed that he wore a tight white suit and a helmet, giving him "a most hideous and frightful appearance." His eyes looked like "red balls of fire," and he shot blue flames from his mouth. Spring-heeled Jack grabbed Miss Alsop and started tearing at her gown with his metal claws. She screamed, managed to break away, and slammed the door shut in his face. Then, in a bizarre twist, Spring-heeled Jack knocked several more times at the door. Why he should think that Alsop would open up again after such treatment is perhaps the greatest mystery of all!

After a time, sightings in London died away, only to revive in 1843. This time many of the sightings came from outside the city. Spring-heeled Jack soon became an iconic figure of popular culture, becoming the star of plays and musicals and the "penny dreadfuls", a form of cheap pulp literature at the time.

THE BOY'S STANDARD.

Published Weekly.   NOW READY.   Price One Penny.

NOS. 1 AND 2 (TWENTY-FOUR PAGES), SPLENDIDLY ILLUSTRATED, IN HANDSOME WRAPPER.

SPRING HEELED JACK.
THE TERROR OF LONDON

The History of this Remarkable Being has been specially compiled, for this work only, by one of the Best Authors of the day, and our readers will find that he has undoubtedly succeeded in producing a Wonderful and Sensational Story, every page of which is replete with details of absorbing and thrilling interest.

A contemporary penny dreadful

Unfortunately, the legend inspired some real-life imitators. In 1855 in Hertford, the body of a young girl was found with scratches on her breasts and shoulders and burns on her legs. At first, people blamed Spring-heeled Jack, who also burnt and scratched his victims, but later a local man confessed, saying he killed the girl because she rejected him.

The sightings died down again, only to return in the 1870s. His favorite place to prowl was now Sheffield, where in April and May of 1873 he terrorized the area and prompted crowds numbering in the hundreds to go out and try hunting him down.

One of the most notable sightings occurred at Aldershot Barracks, a large garrison between the towns of Aldershot and Farnborough in Hampshire. One night in August 1877, a sentry spotted a dark figure leaping along the road towards him. The soldier issued a challenge, which was ignored. The figure then leaped out of view. Confused, the sentry turned back to his post, only to come face to face with Spring-heeled Jack. The soldier described the figure as tall and muscular, wearing some sort of helmet and a white, tight-fitting suit of oilskin. The intruder gave the soldier several slaps on the face with "a hand as cold as that of a corpse." The terrified soldier shouted for help, and when some of his comrades arrived, Spring-heeled Jack leapt right over their heads to land behind them. He then just stood there grinning, as if he was challenging them to do something. One of the soldiers did his duty, leveled his gun, and fired at the intruder. Spring-heeled Jack didn't seem injured by the shot, but he did get angry and charged at the soldiers, breathing blue fire at them. The soldiers scattered and the apparition made his escape.

Spring-heeled Jack returned to Aldershot several times, scaring the sentries, daring them to shoot at him, and always managing to elude capture. Soon Spring-heeled Jack was enjoying his biggest wave of sightings yet, with dozens of reports coming in each month from all over the country. In Lincolnshire, a mob chased him as he leapt over several houses. Witnesses described him as wearing a sheepskin, an odd detail that doesn't come up in other reports. When some of the men in the crowd fired at him, the bullets rang off of him with the sound of something hitting "a hollow bucket." Spring-heeled Jack appeared unharmed as he leaped over some houses and got away.

The sightings continued into the following decade. The *Birmingham Post* reported on him in September 1886, stating breathlessly that, "First a young girl, then a man, felt a hand on their shoulder, and turned to see the infernal one with glowing face, bidding them a good evening."

While the panic gradually subsided, it never entirely went away. There were sightings as late as 1904 in Liverpool, where he was spotted on the roof of Saint Francis Xavier's Church wearing an egg-shaped helmet and laughing at the crowd. He was seen again in 1926 in Bradford.

For a time it seemed old Jack had hung up his springs, and people began to forget about him, but then in 1986 a traveler in South Herefordshire spotted a man in what he described as a "black ski suit" making impossible leaps along the road. The figure had a strangely elongated chin but otherwise looked human. When he got up to the eyewitness, he slapped him across the face and continued on his leaping way. It certainly does sound like Spring-heeled Jack was up to his old tricks again.

There remains no explanation for this odd figure. Could it all have been an invention by the press, which whipped up such hysteria that people came forward with their own "sightings", thus perpetuating the story for the better part of a century? That stretches credulity. Another possibility is that some devious trickster went about scaring people in London and the Home Counties, and that his tricks became embellished in the telling so that he was soon seen everywhere doing superhuman things. It's significant that even during the hysteria of the 19th century, many people thought that Spring-heeled Jack was a human in a suit, not a demon in the flesh but a criminal who needed to be thrown in jail.

Historians have mentioned one possible culprit: the Marquess of Waterford. This Irish nobleman had a reputation that was anything but noble. A drunk, a letch, and a gambler, he would take on any challenge for a wager and was said to hate women. He lived in London for much of the first wave of attacks, although he was known to have been at public functions on the nights of some of them. Nevertheless, many historians feel he is at the core of the mystery. As early as 1880, Rev. E. C. Brewer, wrote that the Marquess "used to amuse himself by springing on travellers unawares, to frighten them, and from time to time others have followed his silly example."

The Marquess of Waterford

In 1842, the Marquess remarried and reportedly became a changed man, retiring to his estates in Ireland and giving up his wayward lifestyle to live the quiet life of a country squire. He died in 1859. If he was the originator of the legend of Spring-heeled Jack, he must have inspired copycats because if it was a human prankster, how could the sightings have lasted from 1837-1986? Even if one dismisses the later accounts, we still have a wave of sightings lasting half a century. No one person could have been responsible for them all.

The Devil's Footprints

Some paranormal investigators have made a link between Spring-heeled Jack and an almost contemporary mystery in Devon. The winter of 1855 was a severe one, and on the night of the 8th of February of that year, the ground was blanketed with a thick new layer of snowfall. As the villagers and farmers of Devon came out of their homes that morning, they saw something strange in the snow.

One news report that was sent around the world described the scene: "It appears on Thursday night last, there was a very heavy snowfall in the neighbourhood of Exeter and the South of Devon. On the following morning the inhabitants of the above towns were surprised at discovering the footmarks of some strange and mysterious animal endowed with the power of ubiquity, as the footprints were to be seen in all kinds of unaccountable places – on the tops of houses and narrow walls, in gardens and court-yards, enclosed by high walls and pailings, as well in open fields."

The tracks looked like horseshoes, but they were smaller and could have been made by no known animal. Not only did the creature that made them seem to be able to leap on top of high buildings, pass across wide rivers, and even apparently pass through walls, the tracks ran for more than a hundred miles.

A naturalist who studied the prints found that it had a stride of some eight and a half inches and that the prints appeared almost in front of one another, suggesting a biped rather than a quadruped. What the naturalist couldn't explain was how this creature could pass over walls 14 feet high without disturbing the snow on top, or why the tracks stopped in some places, only to resume hundreds of feet away.

The Reverend G. M. Musgrove wrote to *The Illustrated London News* in a letter published in March 1855 that his parishioners were so scared that the Devil might be abroad that he told them it was a kangaroo. He admitted his deceit in the letter, apparently assuming none of his superstitious flock would read it. Some newspapers did indeed pick up on the kangaroo theory, but the tracks aren't consistent with those of a kangaroo or any animal of this Earth.

Crop Circles

While most of the mysteries covered so far date back at least a century or more, England is able to bring up new ones as well in order to baffle and inspire later generations. Certainly the oddest unexplained phenomenon in recent years is the crop circle.

Starting in Wessex in the late 1970s, farmers began to notice flattened circles in their crops. The plants, usually cereals, would be pressed down in the entire interior of the circle, with the plants making a clockwise or counterclockwise pattern, or sometimes alternating patterns in different layers. In young crops, the plants would be resilient and spring back up after a few days. In nearly ripe crops, this would not happen and the pattern would endure.

Crop circles began to spread, appearing all over England and then Scotland. They began to become more elaborate too. While the usual flattened discs remained the most common form, some added rings, spokes, half-moons, or even more complex patterns, often of precisely correct, complex geometry. They always appeared at night and no one ever saw their makers, although a fair number of locals claimed they saw strange lights hovering over the fields at night, which got the UFOlogists interested.

They got even more interested when some crop circles appeared that seemed to be pictograms or perhaps writing. One enthusiastic UFO researcher even claimed a crop circle pattern spelled out "Let us leave" in ancient Hebrew! There was no comment from England's Rabbinical community.

By the 1990s, several hundred crop circles were appearing each year in England, and examples were cropping up as far away as Russia, Japan, and Canada. Paranormal investigators were having a field day making up theories as to how they were created. The UFOlogists stuck to aliens, while New Age adherents and pagans pointed to ley lines. Some have pointed out that crop circles often appear near ancient sites, and that the patterns may be the spirit of the land reasserting itself in the modern age. Others claim a more "realistic" explanation by saying the government is experimenting with a new technology, perhaps for some sort of flying disc, which leaves marks on the crops. Why this device wouldn't use one of the many experimental testing grounds the Royal Air Force already has in England is another question.

An entire branch of paranormal study called cereology was founded in order to study the phenomenon, and almost 40 years after the first crop circle appeared, the community is still quite large and active. The turn of the millennium saw a sharp rise in the number and complexity of crop circles, with some showing mathematical equations spelled out in the fields. Other designs were complicated fractals. To date, cereologists have logged more than 2,000 shapes in more than 10,000 crop circles worldwide. No doubt many others went unreported.

Meanwhile, ignored by the enthusiasts and much of the general public, the people who made the crop circles had already confessed. Several mischievous men and women had come up with the idea in Wessex and had brought other pranksters in on the joke. In front of TV cameras they demonstrated how to make a crop circle using a board with rope attached to either end. The crop circle maker holds the ropes in each hand, with the board laid flat in front. Then the prankster uses his foot to push the board against the crop, flattening it. He takes a step forward, flattens another section, and so on. Experienced crop circle makers get into a rhythm that looks a lot like a tailor pumping an old fashioned sewing machine, and they can knock out a fair sized circle in a few minutes.

With a bit of care, more elaborate patterns can be created. The pattern is drawn and measured on paper, and then the dimensions are multiplied when making the real thing. A simple peg and tape measure suffice to get the dimensions right. This explains the lights some people have seen the night before crop circles appear—it's a group of eccentric English men and women finding their way in the dark!

These confessions, however, haven't convinced true believers. How, they ask, could a few jokers create so many crop circles, and how have they spread across the globe? And why would they do it anyway, since they rarely take credit for their work? If they are artists, why are so many of their creations no better than the first simple crop circles that appeared in the late 1970s? Wouldn't artists want to one-up each other by creating ever bolder designs? Thus, the theories continue, making crop circles a very English mystery, at least for some.

Strange Scottish Creatures

One would think that in such an ancient land as Scotland, all the animals living there would have been cataloged and studied by now, but in the more remote corners of the Highlands and islands, there are stories of strange creatures unknown to science. To be fair, this is the case all around the world, as year after year, reports come flooding in of encounters with strange species that some would call monsters. So many different types of unknown creatures have been reported that an entire science (some would say pseudoscience) has developed to study them. It's called cryptozoology, and the creatures it studies are called cryptids.

Scotland's most famous cryptid, of course, lurks in Loch Ness. The Loch Ness Monster is the world's most famous reputed cryptid, and the glacial lake in Scotland that Nessie allegedly calls home has been producing strange sightings since the early Middle Ages. The 7th century manuscript, *Life of St. Columba,* recounts the adventures of an Irish monk in the region as he converted the pagan Picts and performed miracles, and this early description is worth quoting in full:

> "When the blessed man was staying for some days in the province of the Picts, he found it necessary to cross the River Ness; and, when he came to the bank thereof, he sees some of the inhabitants burying a poor unfortunate little fellow, whom, as those who were burying him themselves reported, some water monster had a little before snatched at as he was swimming, and bitten with a most savage bite, and whose hapless corpse some men who came in a boat to give assistance, though too late, caught hold of by putting out hooks. The blessed man however, on hearing this, directs that some one of his companions shall swim out and bring to him the coble [a type of small fishing boat] that is on the other bank, sailing it across.

> "On hearing this direction of the holy and famous man, Lugne Mocumin, obeying without delay, throws all his clothes except his under-garment, and casts himself into the water.

> "Now the monster, which before was not so much satiated as made eager for prey, was lying hid in the bottom of the river; but perceiving that the water above was disturbed by him who was crossing, suddenly emerged, and, swimming to the man as he was crossing in the middle of the stream, rushed up with a great roar and open mouth.

"Then the blessed man looked on, while all who were there, as well the heathen as even the brethren, were stricken with very great terror; and, with his holy hand raised on high, he formed the saving sign of the cross in the empty air, invoked the Name of God, and commanded the fierce monster, saying, 'Think not to go further, nor touch thou the man. Quick! Go back!'

"Then the beast, on hearing this voice of the Saint, was terrified and fled backward more rapidly than he came, as if dragged by cords, although before it had come so near to Lugne as he swam, that there was not more than the length of one punt-pole between the man and the beast. Then the brethren, seeing that the beast had gone away, and that their comrade Lugne was returned to them safe and sound in the boat, glorified God in the blessed man, greatly marveling. Moreover also the barbarous heathens who were there present, constrained by the greatness of that miracle, which they themselves had seen, magnified the God of the Christians."

The careful reader will notice that this encounter occurred on the River Ness, one of the rivers that feeds the loch, and not the loch itself. While many skeptics have used this fact to dismiss the tale of St. Columba, in fact there have been several Nessie sightings on this river.

Between the Middle Ages and the Modern Age there were few sightings except for a smattering of accounts in the 19th century. A wave of sightings in the 1930s brought international attention to the loch and the beast has made countless appearances ever since.

The first photo claiming to be of the creature was taken in 1933, and hundreds more have been taken since then. Most show only a vague shape in the water, looking like one or more dark humps rising from the surface. A few show a long neck with a relatively small head. The most famous and iconic picture, the so-called Surgeon's Photograph taken in 1934, was proven a fake when one of the people who helped take it made a deathbed confession. Many other, similar, photos have yet to be debunked.

The main theory to explain this phenomenon is that Nessie is a plesiosaur, a type of marine dinosaur that supposedly died out 65 million years ago. The general description of Nessie, with its long neck and small head, its humped back, large fins, and long tail, tally well with fossils of plesiosaurs. Several of the better photographs seem to show such a creature. How these animals survived for so long is a mystery. During much of the time that plesiosaurs are known to have lived, this region of Scotland was under water. A plesiosaur fossil dating back 150 million years was discovered at Loch Ness in 2003, but the loch itself wasn't carved out until the last Ice Age 12,000 years ago. How the creature got into the lake is another mystery.

The famous Loch Ness monster hoax photograph of 1934

Accounts of the monster vary depending on how clearly and from what distance the beast was spotted, but they generally agree on the basic details. One very clear sighting on July 22, 1933 by George Spicer and his wife describes how they were driving along the lakeside road (which had only been built earlier that year, bringing more people to the formerly isolated loch) and saw the creature cross their path and slip into the water. Its body was about 4 feet (1.2 m) high and 25 feet (7.6 m) long. Much of this length was taken up by the narrow neck, which Spicer described as being a bit thicker than an elephant's trunk. It was as long as the road was wide, making it about 12 feet (4 m) long. It was sinuous and undulating as the creature moved. A dip in the road kept the Spicers from seeing the bottom of its body, so they could not say if the creature had fins or feet.

That same year, veterinary student Arthur Grant claimed he saw it while on his motorcycle late one night. While he didn't get a good view owing to the darkness, he described the creature as looking like a cross between a plesiosaur and a seal. Grant's testimony is significant because he had zoological knowledge.

10 years later, during World War II, another trained observer claimed he spotted Nessie. This was C. B. Farrel of the Royal Observer Corps, a civil defense unit that kept an eye out for Luftwaffe planes. He saw a creature that was 20-30 feet (6-9 meters) long with fins and a neck that stuck out about 5 feet (1.5 meters) from the water. Farrel took a considerable risk in making his report, because this was the height of the Blitz and his superior officers were understandably on edge and would have had little patience for such things as lake monsters.

Since the early wave of sightings in the 1930s and '40s, there has been a steady number of reports, photographs, and films ever since. What is remarkable is how consistent they are about the general shape and size of the creature. There have also been sonar contacts by various researchers who have detected large objects moving about deep in the water. Recently, however, there has been some concern that the Loch Ness Monster may be going extinct. Sightings have been dropping off seriously in the first decade of the 21st century. A sonar sweep in 2003 failed to detect any underwater presence.

Luckily for the monster and the local economy, 2015 was a bumper year for Nessie sightings, with five officially recognized sightings. Two of the sightings included photographic evidence and two were seen by multiple witnesses. The cryptozoologists, who make it their business to document sightings around the Scottish loch for the Official Loch Ness Monster Sightings Register, consider a sighting official if it defies easy explanation.

Unlike many cryptozoologists, many of the more prominent Nessie experts are scientifically minded skeptics and dismiss many sightings as waves or logs. With so many tourists coming to Loch Ness every year, bringing an estimated £30 million ($43 million) to the region every year, people are going to see what they want to see.

The first sighting of 2015 occurred on April 22, when a couple visiting the historic Urquhart Castle on the shores of the loch saw what they thought looked like a large dolphin emerge from the water, only to quickly slip beneath the surface. This was repeated four to six times before the creature finally disappeared. Another person who didn't know the couple also saw the creature.

Just a few days later on April 25, Dee Bruce and Les Stuart were driving along the shore road when they saw Nessie come about three feet out of the water near the north end of the loch before quickly disappearing again.

On July 1, Crystal Ardito was riding in a boat on the loch when she saw a strange shape in the water and photographed it. It was visible for only a few seconds and she could not clearly see what it was. When she later examined the photo, she zoomed in and saw a grayish object poking out of the water. It was distant and thus quite pixilated, but it appears to be a gray mass atop another gray mass. True believers would say that it was Nessie's neck and hump moving away from the photographer, but it could really be just about anything.

On August 13, Mr. & Mrs. Bates took several photos of a strange undulating mass moving across the water just off from the Loch Ness Holiday Park. It was visible for about five minutes and five other people also saw it. It did not look like a wave, which wouldn't have lasted long anyway, but since nothing ever surfaced, it is difficult to say exactly what it was.

All of these sightings took place in daytime in clear conditions, and Gary Campbell, the keeper of the register, and Steve Feltham, who has been keeping a nearly daily watch over the loch for

25 years, say that while they used to believe in the plesiosaur theory, they now think the monster is actually a giant catfish or eel, or to be more precise a small population of such fish that were introduced into the loch in Victorian times.

Anthony Sheils' photo purported to depict the Loch Ness Monster.

Perhaps not surprisingly, Loch Ness isn't the only Scottish loch to harbor a monster. There are several more lochs with tales to tell. The most active monster besides Nessie resides in Loch Morar, about 70 miles southwest of Loch Ness. The loch is certainly big enough to hide a monster, being a little more than 10 square miles in size and more than 1,000 feet deep, making it the deepest body of fresh water in the British Isles.

John Haynes' picture of Loch Morar

Like the other lochs in the Scottish Highlands, it was created as a result of glacial action about 10,000 years ago, but unlike Loch Ness, which has become built up in recent decades, Loch Morar has retained much of its rugged charm. Few people live along its shores, but that doesn't stop the occasional monster sighting, however. Locals refer to the creature in the loch as Morag.

Morag sightings date back to the 19th century and have continued up to the present time-- investigators have counted 34 sightings, 16 of which have involved more than one eyewitness. The most dramatic encounter came in 1969, when Duncan McDonnell and William Simpson were out fishing in their motorboat one evening. When Simpson went below to make some tea, McDonnell stayed at the helm. As he steered the boat over the loch's placid waters, he heard a loud splash to one side of the boat. Turning his head, he saw a dark form in the water, coming straight for the boat.

A moment later it struck, and Simpson yelled out from below as the teakettle fell off the portable stove. Frightened, McDonnell hurried over to the object and hit it with an oar. As he did, he got a good look at it. The creature was 20, perhaps 30 feet long, with rough, dirty brown skin. McDonnell hit it so hard that his oar broke in two, but had no discernible effect on the monster. McDonnell called for Simpson to bring up his gun from below, which he did, his eyes growing wide at the sight of the thing crashing into the boat. Simpson took a shot at it from point blank range.

Whether the bullet injured Morag or not, they never knew, but at least the creature swam off, disappearing under the water without overturning their boat.

Duncan McDonnell must have been especially shaken at this encounter. The area around Loch Morar is the traditional land of his own McDonnell clan, and it is said that the monster appears whenever a member of the clan is about to die. This legend has been around for centuries. There's even an old folk song about it:

> "Morag, Harbinger of Death
>
> Giant swimmer in deep-green Morar
>
> The loch that has no bottom
>
> There it is that Morag the monster lives."

Luckily for Duncan McDonnell, he survived the encounter, and lived for many more years. It seems the monster is only a prophet of death, not the instigator of it.

One interesting fact about Morag is that it was the first of its kind to be seriously studied by an academic. Around 1902, renowned folklorist Alexander Carmichael stayed by the loch, gathering local legends about its mysterious inhabitant. In one account, Morag isn't a Nessie-style monster at all, but more like a mermaid, with feminine features, flowing golden hair, prominent breasts, and a fish's tail. In this form, too, Morag was the harbinger of death, wailing and swimming around the loch whenever a McDonnell was soon to die. The local people hated and feared her in equal measure.

Carmichael

Morag was also the subject of a determined search that rivaled any of the larger, more famous Loch Ness expeditions in its tenacity and scientific rigor. For several summers in the 1970s, a team of volunteers, led by Adrian Shine, spent several summers trying to find the monster.

Their efforts were aided by the fact that Loch Morar has relatively clear water, unlike Loch Ness's peaty murk. Shine's team placed numerous buoys around the loch with cameras hanging by a line below the surface. The team also installed a pair of television cameras, well below the surface and pointing upwards, in the hope of filming a silhouette of the monster as it swam above, backlit by the sunlight. Sadly, they never caught so much as a glimpse of Morag, and the mystery of what might be in Loch Morar remains unsolved.

Over at Loch Shiel, a few miles south of Loch Morar, the locals talk of Seileag, a creature long enough that it can put up to seven humps above the water at the same time, and has a long neck which ends in a small head with a wide mouth. One report from 1870 puts it at 70 feet in length.

Sightings have been rare because the loch has been isolated for most of recorded history, but the expansion of tourism in the 1990s led to a rise in sightings. One eyewitness claims to have seen four creatures at the same time.

Loch Shiel

Then there's the rarely seen monster at Loch Oich, which, like Loch Shiel, lies just to the south of Loch Ness. This creature has a head like a shaggy dog at the end of a serpentine neck. Its skin is black, and like other lake monsters, it wriggles through the water, showing several humps along its length. Unlike most lake monsters, this one's dangerous. Legend says that some children were playing by the shoreline one day when they saw the monster. One boy decided to show off his bravery and swim out to it to clamber on the creature's back. This only served to frighten the monster, and it dove out of sight, taking the poor child with it.

Claire Pegram's picture of Loch Oich

In the northwest Highlands is Loch Maree, 11 square miles in size and up to 375 feet deep. The loch is the domain of the Muc-sheilche, a creature that looks similar to its cousins in other lochs, although some sightings make it sound like a giant eel. The meaning of its name is open to question, but some think it's Old Gaelic for "slug pig," which is hardly a flattering title. Back in the 1850s, a Mr. Banks got a chip on his shoulder about there being a monster in the loch and decided to get rid of it. He paid vast sums of money trying to drain Loch Maree, but ultimately failed. Then he poured quicklime into the loch to try and poison poor old Muc-sheilche. This didn't work either because Muc-sheilche was spotted soon thereafter, alive and well. Because the loch is so remote, there are few sightings of this beastie, and no one else has tried to kill it since. It's worth a visit, not only for its monster, but also for its rugged beauty and wealth of local legends, such as the old, abandoned chapel and ancient groves on some of the islands, said to have been used by the Druids, and a holy well whose waters can cure madness. Apparently Mr. Banks did not avail himself of this.

Loch Maree

    Investigators have come up with a host of explanations as to what exactly is swimming in all of these lochs. A leading theory is that it is a plesiosaur, a type of marine dinosaur that supposedly died out 65 million years ago in the great dinosaur extinction at the end of the Cretaceous Period. The descriptions of the loch monsters, with their thick bodies, long necks, and relatively small heads, certainly sound like the description of a plesiosaur, but the lochs are much, much more recent than the last known plesiosaur, having been scoured out during the last Ice Age only 10,000 years ago.

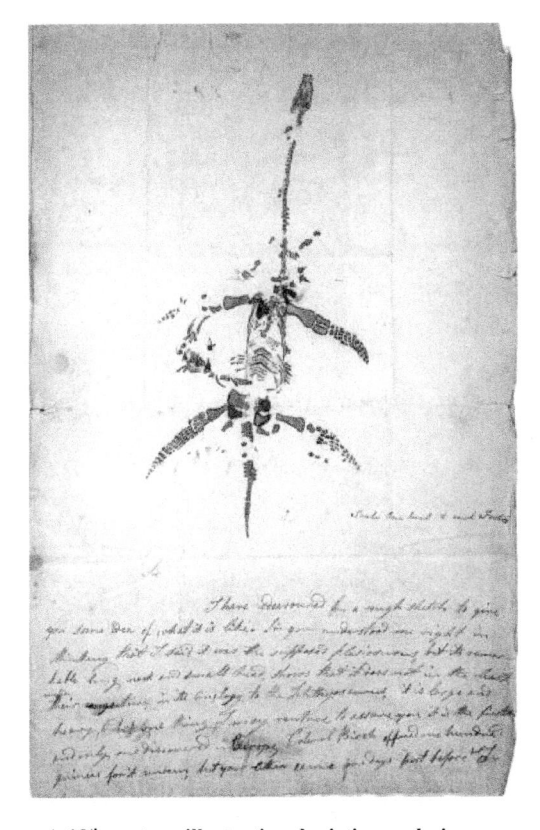

A 19th century illustration depicting a plesiosaur

Another explanation is that they are giant eels. Eels have been proven to live in Loch Ness and Morar, but they usually only reach a few feet in length. At times, however, eels are born sterile, and these tend to grow much larger. The only problem with this theory is that reports consistently state that the loch monsters undulate up and down and will lift their heads out of the water. Eels undulate side to side like snakes, and do not lift their heads out of the water.

All of these loch monsters might leave the impression that if one stays away from large bodies of water, one will be safe from cryptids, but nothing could be further from the truth. Besides the various spirits and fairies that flit over the land, which will be further discussed below, there are also certain strange species that could very well be unknown animals.

The most common are the so-called Alien Big Cats, which cryptozoologists affectionately refer to as ABCs. Alien Big Cats aren't monsters; instead, they appear to be known species, such as tigers and panthers, found in places they shouldn't be, like in Scotland. Large predators have been extinct in Scotland for centuries, but there are persistent reports of large felines stalking the moors and fields of Scotland.

At least one ABC has been captured in Scotland. Through much of the late 1970s, people in Inverness-shire reported seeing a puma wandering through the countryside. Newspapers either printed hyped-up reports or laughed it off. Then the mysterious puma became real news when, in 1980, a farmer named Ted Noble set up a cage trap and managed to capture it. It was given to the Highland Wildlife Park Zoo, where experts noted its docile nature and theorized it had been brought up domesticated and released into the countryside when it grew too large. The puma has since died, and can now be seen, proudly stuffed, in the Inverness Museum.

There may be more out there. In 2006, a large black cat was filmed on the outskirts of Banff, Aberdeenshire. From the footage (easily found on YouTube), it appears to be a very large black cat, although it's difficult to say whether it's an oversized housecat or a panther. Numerous eyewitnesses who have seen the cat over the years insist that it isn't a regular tomcat, but rather something a bit wilder and much bigger.

In 2009, in Helensburgh, Argyll, another video surfaced of a purported ABC, and this time it was from as professional a witness as anyone could hope for: a Ministry of Defense police dog handler. On June 30, Police Constable Chris Swallow was working on a garden overlooking a railway line when he spotted a large, black feline, as big as a Labrador. Though it is a bit pixelated and shaky, the one-minute video clearly shows a feline with a body as long as the gauge of the tracks, which in Scotland are 4' 8.5". In the video, the tail is never extended so it's impossible to estimate the animal's entire length, but even so, it is clearly not a house cat.

This is an area well known for Alien Big Cat sightings, the most famous being the Coulport Cougar, a large, tan feline, seen in the woods and hills starting in June 2004, with numerous reports in the following years. A large, black cat has also been seen, and this might be what PC Swallow filmed.

The Big Cats in Britain Group, which collects reports on ABCs, lists more than 20 sightings a year from Argyll, and a few hundred across the country.

A more serious encounter happened in Ayrshire, just a few weeks after PC Swallow's sighting. On July 22, the *Daily Mail* printed an article titled "Big Cat Attack on Horse puts Parents on Guard at Holiday Park." The paper reported that local police had put parents on alert to mind their children after a horse was attacked in the night, suffering long, raking, claw wounds that a local veterinarian thought had come from a puma, or some other feline predator. A sandy-colored puma, measuring 6 feet long, spotted in the area earlier that summer, was thought to be the culprit. Even the superintendent of the Ayr police office thought that a puma could be responsible, noting that in May, the staff at Sundrum Castle had seen what looked like a four foot high, six foot long puma, on the castle grounds.

The attack happened, frightfully enough, right next to Sundrum Holiday Park, a caravan park where holidaymakers were sleeping.

Given these headlines, those who go hiking in Scotland may want to keep a sharp eye out for panthers and pumas. One can't be too careful in the wild, though it's always helpful to remember that feline predators rarely attack humans. Those seeking to lessen their chances of being a newsworthy exception should raise their hands and stand tall, making themselves as big as possible, while backing off slowly, and shouting. Do not approach the animal, but feel free to film it from a safe distance and pass along more evidence about the Alien Big Cats.

The Horrible History of Sawney Beane

SAWNEY BEANE at the Entrance of his Cave

A contemporary depiction of Sawney Beane at the entrance of his cave

While many cynics might scoff at tales of cryptids in lochs and pumas in holiday parks, Scotland has definitely been the abode of real monsters. What's even worse, these monsters were human.

The *Newgate Calendar*, a popular summary of terrible crimes that circulated in the 18th century, is filled with ghastly tales of murder and cruelty, but none are more terrible than the tale of Sawney Beane and his family of cannibalistic serial killers. The story was widely popular when it was published, and was kept in print for more than a century. The *Newgate Calendar* related the following:

> "SAWNEY BEANE was born in the county of East Lothian, about eight or nine miles eastward of the city of Edinburgh, some time in the reign of Queen Elizabeth, whilst King James I governed only in Scotland. [i.e.: sometime between 1567 to 1603, although more likely in the latter part of this period].

> "…being very much prone to idleness, and not caring for being confined to any honest employment, he left his father and mother, and ran away into the desert part of the country, taking with him a woman as viciously inclined as himself. These two took up their habitation in a rock by the seaside, on the shore of the county of Galloway, where they lived upwards of twenty-five years without going into any city, town, or village.

> "In this time they had a great number of children and grandchildren, whom they brought up after their own manner, without any notions of humanity or civil society. They never kept any company but among themselves, and supported themselves wholly by robbing; being, moreover, so very cruel, that they never robbed anyone whom they did not murder.

> "By this bloody method, and their living so retiredly from the world, they continued such a long time undiscovered, there being nobody able to guess how the people were lost that went by the place where they lived. As soon as they had robbed and murdered any man, woman or child, they used to carry off the carcass to the den, where, cutting it into quarters, they would pickle the mangled limbs, and afterwards eat it; this being their only sustenance. And, notwithstanding, they were at last so numerous, they commonly had superfluity of this their abominable food; so that in the night time they frequently threw legs and arms of the unhappy wretches they had murdered into the sea, at a great distance from their bloody habitation. The limbs were often cast up by the tide in several parts of the country, to the astonishment and terror of all the beholders, and others who heard it. Persons who had gone about their lawful occasions fell so often into their hands that it caused a general outcry in the

country round about, no man knowing what was become of his friend or relation, if they were once seen by these merciless cannibals."

The *Newgate Calendar* noted that the locals soon began to fear for their lives, and set upon any stranger as a possible culprit. Also, any innkeeper so unfortunate as to host travelers before they disappeared would be lynched, the mob thinking they had found the murderer.

Sadly, they soon discovered their mistake when more body parts washed ashore. The *Newgate Calendar* goes on:

> "Sawney's family was at last grown very large, and every branch of it, as soon as able, assisted in perpetrating their wicked deeds, which they still followed with impunity. Sometimes they would attack four, five or six foot men together, but never more than two if they were on horseback. They were, moreover, so careful that not one whom they set upon should escape, that an ambuscade was placed on every side to secure them, let them fly which way they would, provided it should ever so happen that one or more got away from the first assailants. How was it possible they should be detected, when not one that saw them ever saw anybody else afterwards? The place where they inhabited was quite solitary and lonesome; and when the tide came up, the water went for near two hundred yards into their subterraneous habitation, which reached almost a mile underground; so that when some who had been sent armed to search all the by-places about had passed by the mouth of their cave, they had never taken any notice of it, not supposing that anything human would reside in such a place of perpetual horror and darkness.

> "The number of the people these savages destroyed was never exactly known, but it was generally computed that in the twenty-five years they continued their butcheries they had washed their hands in eke blood of a thousand, at least, men, women and children. The manner how they were at last discovered was as follows.

> "A man and his wife behind him on the same horse coming one evening home from a fair, and falling into the ambuscade of these merciless wretches, they fell upon them in a most furious manner. The man, to save himself as well as he could, fought very bravely against them with sword and pistol, riding some of them down, by main force of his horse. In the conflict the poor woman fell from behind him, and was instantly murdered before her husband's face; for the female cannibals cut her throat and fell to sucking her blood with as great a gust as if it had been wine. This done, they ripped up her belly and pulled out all her entrails. Such a dreadful spectacle made the man make the more obstinate resistance, as expecting the same fate if he fell into their hands. It pleased Providence, while he was engaged, that twenty or thirty from the same fair came together in a body; upon which Sawney Beane and his bloodthirsty clan withdrew, and made the best of their way through a

thick wood to their den.

"This man, who was the first that had ever fallen in their way and came off alive, told the whole company what had happened, and showed them the horrid spectacle of his wife, whom the murderers had dragged to some distance, but had not time to carry her entirely off. They were all struck with stupefaction and amazement at what he related, took him with them to Glasgow, and told the affair to the provost of that city, who immediately sent to the King concerning it.

"…his Majesty himself in person, with a body of about four hundred men, set out for the place where this dismal tragedy was acted, in order to search all the rocks and thickets, that, if possible, they might apprehend this hellish cure, which had been so long pernicious to all the western parts of the kingdom.

"The man who had been attacked was the guide, and care was taken to have a large number of bloodhounds with them, that no human means might be wanting towards their putting an entire end to these cruelties.

"No sign of any habitation was to be found for a long time, and even when they came to the wretches' cave they took no notice of it, but were going to pursue their search along the seashore, the tide being then out. But some of the bloodhounds luckily entered this Cimmerian den, and instantly set up a most hideous barking, howling and yelping; so that the King, with his attendants, came back, and looked into it. They could not yet tell how to conceive that anything human could be concealed in a place where they saw nothing but darkness. Never the less, as the bloodhounds increased their noise, went farther in, and refused to come back again, they began to imagine there was some reason more than ordinary. Torches were now immediately sent for, and a great many men ventured in through the most intricate turnings and windings, till at last they arrived at that private recess from all the world which was the habitation of these monsters.

"Now the whole body, or as many of them as could, went in, and were all so shocked at what they beheld that they were almost ready to sink into the earth. Legs, arms, thighs, hands and feet of men, women and children were hung up in rows, like dried beef. A great many limbs lay in pickle, and a great mass of money, both gold and silver, with watches, rings, swords, pistols, and a large quantity of clothes, both linen and woollen, and an infinite number of other things, which they had taken from those whom they had murdered, were thrown together in heaps, or hung up against the sides of the den.

"Sawney's family at this time, besides him, consisted of his wife, eight sons, six daughters, eighteen grandsons, and fourteen granddaughters, who were all begotten in incest.

"These were all seized and pinioned by his Majesty's order in the first place; then they took what human flesh they found and buried it in the sands; afterwards loading themselves with the spoils which they found, they returned to Edinburgh with their prisoners, all the country, as they passed along, flocking to see this cursed tribe. When they were come to their journey's end, the wretches were all committed to the Tolbooth, from whence they were the next day conducted under a strong guard to Leith, where they were all executed without any process, it being thought needless to try creatures who were even professed enemies to mankind.

"The men had their hands and legs severered from their bodies; by which amputations they bled to death in some hours. The wife, daughters and grandchildren, having been made spectators of this just punishment inflicted on the men, were afterwards burnt to death in three several fires. They all in general died without the least signs of repentance; but continued cursing and venting the most dreadful imprecations to the very last gasp of life."

It's a truly gruesome tale, but some historians question its veracity. For example, if King James had personally led a mission against them, it would have surely been written up in detail in the royal chronicle, and yet there is no record of it. On the other hand, the region was known for its lawlessness at the time, and numerous cases of cannibalism are recorded in the crime annals.

Moreover, the tale of Sawney Beane was reported in other publications. The *Newgate Calendar* often exaggerated its tales for emphasis (and to sell copies), but is known to be broadly factual.

As has been made too apparent throughout history, there are enough sick people in the world that there is no need to make up such stories. In all likelihood, Sawney Beane and his anthropophagic family did exist, though their grisly deeds may have been embellished over time. Perhaps they killed and ate "only" a few dozen people rather than several hundred.

Scottish Ghosts and Spirits

Scotland is an ancient land that has seen much tragedy in its bloody history. Many of the buildings that witnessed those tragedies still survive, so it should come as no surprise that it's considered one of the most haunted countries in the world.

The hauntings start just as visitors get to the border between England and Scotland. Berwick-upon-Tweed is located just over two miles south of the current border in the English county of Northumberland, and it has been fought over by the English and Scots for centuries. For much of its history, Berwick-upon-Tween was a Scottish town, and many believe it is still home to a very Scottish ghost.

Berwick Castle, which dates back to Norman times and was the scene of much of the fighting, now stands in ruins, but at least one old occupant allegedly still resides there. On moonlit nights, some people have seen a Highland bagpiper in full regalia, standing atop the crumbled battlements, playing a ghostly tune. He is most often seen standing close to a steep flight of stone steps, locally referred to as "the breakneck stairs." Is the piper commemorating the accidental death of some long-departed Scot--perhaps himself?

An 18th century depiction of Berwick Castle

The ruins of the castle today

The piper isn't the only ghost in Berwick-upon-Tweed. All three bridges spanning the River Tweed have their own ghosts. The oldest bridge, named Berwick Bridge, or by the local and not particularly original name of Old Bridge, was built in the early 17th century. At times the gray, blurry figure of a hooded monk can be seen walking across this historic span.

The Royal Border Bridge is a railway bridge built by famous railway engineer Robert Stephenson in 1850 at the dawn of the railway era. He was the son of George Stephenson, who built the world's first inter-city railway line between Liverpool and Manchester, in 1830. Robert Stephenson followed in the footsteps of his father and helped the railroad crisscross England. The Royal Border Bridge is one of his masterpieces, being 2,162 ft (659 m) long, with 28 arches rising 121 ft (37 m) above the river. Robert died in 1859, and has often been seen since, stalking the railway bridge at night, still admiring his creation.

Robert Stephenson

A third bridge, opened in 1928, is haunted by the ghost of a worker who died during its construction. It is one of the many constructions worldwide that are home to spirits of the men who died while building them.

In Scotland proper, the ghosts seemingly only get thicker. On the border, they tend to stick to travel routes and old buildings, and there are even entire stretches of roads that are considered haunted. The most notorious is the A75, especially the Kinmount Straight section in southwest Scotland, locally known as the "Ghost Road." This stretch of highway has seen numerous paranormal encounters for more than half a century.

The earliest sighting dates to 1957, when a truck driver passing along the A75 at night saw a couple walking, arm in arm, right across the road in front of him. He slammed on his brakes and was convinced he'd hit them. Once he'd pulled over, he jumped out of his vehicle to search for the bodies, but the couple had vanished.

A more dramatic apparition happened in 1962, when Derek and Norman Ferguson were driving along the road at around midnight. Suddenly, a large hen flapped up towards their windshield. The two men were startled, but not spooked. Anyone who has spent time driving in rural areas has had at least one near miss, thanks to a stray farm animal. Chasing after the hen came an old woman, waving her arms at the car. At first, the two men thought this was the owner of the animal, but then their experience got weirder. Right behind the old woman came a screaming man with long hair, followed closely by a menagerie of wild dogs, giant cats, hens, goats, and some creatures the Fergusons couldn't identify.

They didn't have long to look, as all of the people and the creatures disappeared in an instant. By this time, they had stopped the car. Suddenly, they felt the temperature plunge, and the car began to rock violently from side to side as if by an unseen force. Derek, either bravely or foolishly, got out of the car and the movement stopped as abruptly as it had started. He got back in, shaken and bewildered, only to see a large van come barreling down the street at them. It vanished just before hitting them.

The detail about the temperature going down is an interesting one. Paranormal investigators believe that ghosts draw ambient energy from the air around them, which causes the temperature to plunge. The more energy they require, the more the temperature will go down. The Fergusons felt the temperature go down quickly, just before the unseen spirits rocked their car. Some specialists in the spirits of the dead theorize that a ghost's need for energy is one of the reasons they are so rarely seen during the daytime. The power of the sun overwhelms them, it being too powerful for them to manifest in their weakened state, and thus blanks them out.

It's interesting that the ghosts that came at the Fergusons seemed to be trying to communicate with the land of the living. Garson and Monica Miller were driving at around 60 mph along the road one night in March of 1995, when suddenly a man stepped out, right in front of them. He looked to be middle aged, but rather strange. He had an empty sack folded on top of his head, and held what appeared to be a rag in his hands as he outstretched his arms towards the car. They didn't get much of a look, because they were going too fast. Like other drivers on this stretch of road, they were convinced they had hit what they'd thought was a regular human being, but when they screeched to a halt and went back to look, there was, of course, no trace of him. The couple was so concerned, they filed a police report.

The police received another baffling report in July of 1997, when Donna Maxwell was driving along the A75 with her two children. As with the other apparitions, a man stepped out into the road, right in front of her. Maxwell described him as being in his 30s with short hair, a red top, and dark pants. He, too, disappeared upon impact. She filed a police report, and apparently was so convincing, that the police didn't dismiss her story, but rather, issued a description of the man, asking the public for any clues. No one had seen the incident or reported a man with that description who had been injured in a car accident.

In another encounter back in 2012, a long-distance truck driver had parked on the Kinmount Straight portion of the A75, and took a nap in the back of his truck. The fellow must not have been a local, because no one familiar with the area would have ever considered doing that! He woke up at three in the morning with a dreadful sense of foreboding. When he looked out the window, he saw a long column of bedraggled people in what appeared to be medieval peasants' rags. Some were pushing handcarts as they trudged down the road like refugees. Others have seen this grim cavalcade, too.

The medieval refugees seem to be the only repeat performers on the A75. While hauntings in most places are typified by the same ghost appearing again and again, like the ghostly piper of Berwick Castle, the A75 ghosts are unusual for their variety, including everything from hens to eyeless phantoms.

The hauntings on the A75 Kinmount Straight fall into a pattern seen on many haunted roadways in the British Isles. Phantom travelers who suddenly disappear have been a part of road lore, probably as long as there have been roads, but with the invention of the automobile, they took on a different flavor. Now, instead of a farmer meeting a ghostly apparition at night while walking home from the May Fair or harvesting, a motorist will catch a glimpse of a ghost and think they have run it over. When they go to investigate, the ghost has disappeared. The A75 Kinmount Straight is not the only haunted road in Scotland, but it is the quintessential one.

If the A75 is the most haunted road in Scotland, Edinburgh must be the most haunted city. This ancient center of Scottish life has been witness to some of the great events of Scottish history, and at the same time, has been a place of misery for many common people.

The city's most conspicuous landmark is Edinburgh Castle, sitting high atop a rocky eminence that dominates the surrounding countryside. It is a truly magnificent sight, having served as a defensive position since Celtic times, from at least the 2nd century AD. It started off being a fortress for the kings of Scotland, as early as the reign of King David I (1124-1153). Like many Scottish castles, it was the scene of bitter fighting on numerous occasions, having been besieged at least 26 times in its history, and perhaps more, since its early history is poorly known. Now it hosts numerous public events, and is a fascinating historic site where visitors get to see various museum displays, the Crown Jewels of Scotland, and the enormous medieval cannon, Mons Meg.

Kim Traynor's picture of Edinburgh Castle

Much of the paranormal activity in the castle comes in the form of strange sounds. Phantom drummers can be heard at night, calling the men to defend the battlements, and the castle wardens report strange knockings in locked and supposedly empty buildings. There is also a spectral piper who is heard but not seen, and a drummer who almost nobody wants to see because he's missing his head! The spirits manifest in other ways, too, such as sudden drops in temperature. Some people have also said they've felt an invisible hand tugging on their clothing, or touching their face.

Many other landmarks in town are haunted, too. One of the most notorious is the Learmonth Hotel, a 19th century building with an abundance of poltergeist activity. Unlike ghosts who are seen, heard, and sometimes felt, poltergeists are unseen spirits who move objects. The word comes from the German *poltern* ("to make noise") and *Geist* ("ghost" or "spirit"), and that's exactly what the poltergeists at the Learmonth Hotel do. Doors open and shut by themselves, and sometimes the guests get locked out of their rooms so the spirits can play inside, turning on electrical appliances and whistling strange tunes. Staffers have become resigned to the paranormal goings-on and try to reassure the guests that poltergeists rarely actually hurt anyone.

Then there is Edinburgh's fabled underground warren of tunnels and rooms, called the Vaults. These are a series of corridors and connected, vaulted rooms that run under the city, and have been there for at least two hundred years, perhaps longer. Nobody is all that sure, but it appears that, as is the case with the Paris catacombs, they have been added to over the years. The main line of vaults are actually a series of 19 subterranean arches holding up the city's South Bridge, finished in 1788, but the subterranean passageways extend further than that. Some rooms have been sealed off and converted into pubs and underground nightclubs. Others sit empty.

Kjetil Bjørnsrud's pictures of parts of the Vaults

They were not always so. In the 18th and 19th centuries, there were a large number of indigent rural folk who came to Edinburgh, hoping to find a means of making a living, and ended up sleeping in the Vaults for lack of a better shelter. It was cold, it was damp, and it was pitch dark, but at least it was free.

It was also dangerous. Thieves, murderers, and body snatchers prowled the darkness, and many times the poor residents of the Vaults were awoken by pitiful screams of hapless victims. It is said that many of these victims still lurk in the Vaults today, tied to the place where they suffered in life. It is certainly a disconcerting place. The author visited the Vaults one night with a guide and found them cold and clammy, with strange sounds echoing off the stone walls. Since the Vaults run under inhabited buildings and busy roads, sounds get captured and rebound off the stone, intermingling in strange, eerie ways. It is easy to imagine such a place to be haunted.

One room has been converted into the worship center of a local coven of witches. These are not the witches of fable, but modern practitioners of Wicca, a recognized religion that attempts to recreate and preserve the old folk religion of Europe. Some of the 21st century witches had to cast many purification spells against hostile sprits to cleanse their worship area before they could practice their craft in peace, but the witches were only able to clean out their own vault. Others are still the lairs of angry spirits who appear faintly to living visitors, or whose footsteps still echo down the passageways.

Some of the ghosts are said to be the victims of William Burke and William Hare, the two most notorious resurrection men in Scottish history. In the early 19th century, the law made it extremely difficult for surgeons to procure corpses for dissection, so medical students were denied a vital part of their education. To compensate for this, resurrection men dug up the bodies of the recently dead and offered them to medical schools at a price.

Hare and Burke

Burke and Hare were two Irish immigrants who'd worked various jobs before hitting upon this grim mode of making a living. It is unknown how they ended up as friends, but at some point, Burke moved into Hare's home, where he let out spare rooms to lodgers, and the two made an unlikely partnership. Hare was described, by all contemporary accounts, as a drunken brawler, and a brute. Burke was more educated and professed to be a religious man, although he, too, drank to excess.

Both turned out to be cold-blooded killers. Their first crime came by a stroke of luck, as a contemporary broadside recounts: "In December 1827, a man died in Hare's house, whose body they sold to the Anatomists for £10. Getting so much money at a time when they were in a state of poverty, prompted them to look after means of the same kind, and the subject of murder was often talked over betwixt Hare and [Burke]. The first victim was an old woman belonging to Gilmerton, whom Hare had observed intoxicated on the street, and enticed into his house; they stupified her with more whisky, and put her to death in the way they pursued ever afterwards, by covering and pressing upon the nose and mouth with their hands. The body was carried to Surgeon's Square, and the money readily obtained for it."

The two men justified the sale of the body with the fact that the tenant had owed Hare £4. They had no justification for their second victim, another lodger, whom they got drunk and then suffocated.

In total they were charged with murdering 16 people, all of whom were sold to Dr. Robert Knox, a surgeon who used to lecture on human anatomy by dissecting corpses in front of a paying audience. The bodies were delivered in a large tea chest, the two men acting like they were workers with a delivery for the Surgeons' Hall. Many of the victims were lured into Hare's boarding house, given plenty of liquor, and then strangled. One of the victims was a mentally disabled teenage boy.

The two resurrection men also did away with an old woman and her 12 year-old mute grandson. While Hare smothered the old woman, Burke bent the child over his knee and broke his back. Later, while awaiting execution in prison, Burke confessed that this killing troubled him the most of all his crimes, and that he couldn't get the boy's dying expression out of his head. The tea chest they usually used to deliver the victims proved to be too small to fit both bodies, so they used a herring barrel instead. The two resurrection men put it on a cart drawn by Hare's horse, but when the animal wouldn't pull the heavy load up the steep hill to the Surgeons' Hall, they had to hire a third man—who was unaware of the barrel's grisly contents—to help them move it. Once Hare returned home, he was so infuriated with his horse that he shot it.

Burke and Hare generally had to get drunk to get up the courage to commit their crimes. At his trial, Burke confessed that he "could not sleep at night without a bottle of whisky by his bedside, and a twopenny candle to burn all night beside him; when he awoke he would take a draught of the bottle—sometimes half a bottle at a draught—and that would make him sleep." Clearly, his troubled conscience didn't stop him from committing more murders.

That such a series of killings, all in the space of a single year, should go undetected is testament to the misery in which Edinburgh's poor had to live. The victims were mostly indigent, or poor and working jobs such as junk collectors, and the authorities simply didn't care about them. The killings were almost exposed when the body of the mentally disabled young man was delivered to Dr. Knox. Several of the students recognized him because he was a common and well-known figure who'd wandered the streets, but Knox denied it was him and quickly began the dissection, soon making the corpse unrecognizable. The students made no more fuss about the matter.

Dr. Knox

As Sir Walter Scott would later quip, "Our Irish importation have made a great discovery of Oeconomicks, namely, that a wretch who is not worth a farthing while alive, becomes a valuable article when knockd on the head & carried to an anatomist; and acting on this principle, have cleard the streets of some of those miserable offcasts of society, whom nobody missed because nobody wishd to see them again."

The pair only got caught because a pair of Hare's lodgers, who had somehow survived up to this point, stumbled upon one of the murder victims before Burke and Hare could move the body. By the time the police arrived, they had delivered the body to Knox, but they soon broke down under questioning. It wasn't long before both of them were up before a judge.

The court was faced with a problem, however. They did not have firm evidence for any of the killings except the last, and there was no evidence the final victim had died by violence. The court decided to offer Hare to turn King's evidence, making him free from prosecution if he fingered Burke. This he did, and Burke was found guilty, sentenced to hang, and then have his body publicly dissected.

As one broadside dating to 1829 covering the hanging of William Burke gleefully reported, "His struggles were long and violent, and his body was agonizingly convulsed. We observed that his fall was unusually short, scarcely more than three inches, the noose instead of being as is usual, immediately behind his ear, was at the very summit of the vertebrae. We should have mentioned that when the rope was placed about his neck there was a universal cry raised of 'Burke him;' and, during the whole of the horrible process, there were repeated cries of Hare, Hare. A precentor or clerk was upon the scaffold, as it had been arranged that he should exercise his function; but such were the indications of the feelings of the populace, that those in authority saw it prudent to dispense with this part of the ceremony. Great attempts were made by the Magistrates, officers and others in attendance, upon the scaffold, by signals, to silence the mob during the putting up of prayers; but their efforts were altogether ineffectual. At every struggle the wretch made when suspended, a most rapturous shout was raised by the multitude. When the body was cut down, at three quarters past eight, the most frightful yell we ever heard was raised by the indignant populace, who manifested the most eager desire to get the monster's carcase within their clutches, to gratify their revenge, even after the law had been satisfied, by tearing it to pieces. They were only restrained by the bold front presented by the police. We observed the persons under the scaffold, with knives and scissors, possessing themselves of part of the rope and even slipping into their pockets some of the shavings from the coffin. The scramble at this time was of the most extraordinary nature ever witnessed at an execution in this country."

An illustration of Burke's execution

The surgeon who performed the dissection was Professor Alexander Monro, who, ironically enough, was the man Burke and Hare had originally intended to sell their first victim to. By chance, Munro wasn't around when they delivered the body, and so they ended up selling it to Knox. During the dissection, which attracted record crowds, Monro dipped a quill pen into the dead man's blood and wrote "This is written with the blood of Wm Burke, who was hanged at Edinburgh. This blood was taken from his head."

Burke's skull was given to the Edinburgh Phrenological Society for study. Phrenology is a quack medical belief that was popular at that time. It proposed the theory that a person's character and intellect could be perceived by studying the bumps on his head. Burke must have had some fascinating bumps. The residents of Edinburgh were fascinated by his skin too, and they cut it up, tanned it into leather, and used it to make wallets.

Modern visitors can still see relics from this horrible chapter in Edinburgh's history. Burke's skeleton is on display at the Anatomical Museum of the Edinburgh Medical School. The phrenologists eventually tired of fondling the murderer's skull and reunited it with the skeleton for the sake of posterity. Over at the museum housed in Old Surgeons' Hall, yoneou can see his death mask, and a book supposedly bound in his tanned skin. Some of Knox's surgical instruments are also on display. While the Burke skin wallets have all disappeared, a calling card case made from the skin of the back of his left hand is on display at the Cadies & Witchery Tours museum.

Kim Traynor's picture of Old Surgeons' Hall

Despite Burke's inglorious end, his victims have not been able to rest. Locals whisper that some of the screams that can be heard echoing through the Vaults at night are those of the poor people the two men murdered. Others hear the rumble of the resurrection men's cart in the street outside the Old Surgeons' Hall. Perhaps the spirits are restless because Hare got off "Scot-free," and Knox also escaped prosecution because Burke insisted throughout the trial that the surgeon did not know the bodies were those of murder victims. Even the passage of the Anatomy Act of 1832, which made it easier to obtain cadavers for dissection, and which was a direct result of the Burke and Hare murders, did not lay the spirits to rest. To this day they call for justice from beyond the grave.

Other spirits, inhuman ones, travel about the further reaches of Scotland. Fairies, brownies, and merfolk all make Scotland their home, and though fewer people believe in them today than in the old times, some still cling to the belief that they are real, as a housing developer found out as recently as 2005.

In its November 21 edition of that year, *The Times* newspaper reported that a housing development in the village of St Fillans, Perthshire, on the eastern shore of Loch Earn, had been halted over a local concern that it would disturb the fairies. The developer, Marcus Salter of Genesis Properties, was just getting underway, ordering his diggers to start tearing up the land, when a local came running up shouting that he would disturb the fairies. It turned out that a large stone on the land was locally reputed to be a fairy stone. There were wee folk living under it, and if they were disturbed there would be no end of trouble.

Salter dismissed the complaint as being from some crank, but he was soon inundated with irate phone calls and brought before the local council, something no housing developer ever wants to experience. When he revealed that he planned to move the stone to the side of the road and engrave the name of the housing estate on it, the council was not amused, and took the fairy believers' side. One councilwoman frankly told *The Times* that she believed in fairies. Most of her colleagues tried to save face by pointing out that it was an historic spot and should be preserved on that basis. St. Fillan, a Celtic missionary of the sixth century, was said to have had his camp there when he tried to convert the Pagan Picts. The stone is locally believed to have been used as a place to crown the new Pictish king.

Many natural features in the British Isles have these dual historical/folkloric significances attached to them. It's possible that the stone was seen as a source of magic, causing the Pictish kings to hold their coronations there. Alternatively, the fact that it was a place of ancient royal significance could have prompted people to continue to look upon it as having some sort of mystical power, with the idea of it being a home to fairies cropping up later. The belief that a natural or manmade landmark can hold power over a place is a deep-rooted one in the folklore of the British Isles. That a Perthshire councilwoman, an elected official, could tell one of the country's major newspapers that she believed in fairies and that it would be a bad idea to move their home, shows just how tenacious these beliefs are in the modern world.

In the end, Salter was forced to redo his business plans, coming up with a whole new design that would see a garden in the middle of the housing development, with the fairy stone in its usual place as a centerpiece. The developer estimated the fairy furor cost him about £15,000 ($20,000 or 17,900 euros) in replanning costs. It's expensive to mess with fairies.

At least no one tried to burn down Salter's house. In 1814, a newcomer by the name of Captain W. Mackay got into trouble with the local Orkney Islanders off the north coast of Scotland for messing with a standing stone. He had bought land on which stood the so-called Odin Stone, a tall, standing stone with a large hole through it near its base. It stands near the famous stone circle, the Standing Stones of Stenness, which remains an impressive landmark, and well worth a visit. The Orcadians believed the Odin Stone to have magical properties, and on the first few days of the new year, people from all over the islands would come to the stone, camp out, and dance. Many young men and women promised themselves in marriage by standing on opposite sides of the stone and clasping their hands through the hole.

The Standing Stones of Stenness

All of this partying and lovemaking disturbed the captain's land, and he decided to put an end to it by destroying the stone. This he did, and he was setting his sights on the Standing Stones of Stenness and the nearby Ring of Brodgar, another stone circle, when he received a nasty warning from the local islanders. They tried to burn down his house and barns several times, and eventually forced him to flee the area. Sadly, he was able to destroy a couple of the stones at Stenness before he was booted off the island.

Scottish Mysteries

There are plenty of mysterious occurrences in Scotland that don't fit into any tidy category.

One of the more famous happened at the Eilean Mor Lighthouse, on one of the Flannan Islands in the remote and windswept Outer Hebrides, and remains among the most enigmatic disappearances on record. Eilean Mor lies ten miles off the west coast of the Isle of Lewis, and while it hasn't been permanently inhabited since medieval hermits lived there to get away from civilization and search for God, it has long had a lighthouse on it to guide ships through the stormy waters and hidden rocks along one of the most dangerous coastlines in Europe. The only people living on the island in the modern day have been a rotating team of three lighthouse keepers.

The lighthouse

In December of 1900, those keepers were Thomas Marshall, James Ducat, and Donald MacArthur, all experienced, reliable men. The first hint of trouble came on December 15, when the steamer *SS Archtor* passed the island at midnight and did not see the light.

A stretch of bad weather came on, and the relief ship, the *SS Hesperus*, didn't arrive until December 29. The ship approached the landing, expecting one of the keepers to come down and assist their rowboat in docking as usual. This is essential for safety with the tricky waters along the islands. However, no one showed up.

Joseph Moore, a lighthouse keeper who was on the *Hesperus* to relieve one of the men, wrote this report:

"[W]e came to anchorage under Flannan Islands, and not seeing the Lighthouse Flag flying, we thought they did not perceive us coming. The steamer's horn was sounded several times, still no reply. At last Captain Harvie deemed it prudent to lower a boat and land a man if it was possible. I was the first to land leaving Mr. McCormack and his men in the boat till I should return from the lighthouse. I went up, and on coming to the entrance gate I found it closed. I made for entrance door leading to the kitchen and store room, found it also closed and the door inside that, but the kitchen door itself was open. On entering the kitchen I looked at the fireplace and saw that the fire was not lighted for some days. I then entered the rooms in succession, found the beds empty just as they left them in the early morning. I did not take time to search further, for I only too well knew something serious had occurred. I darted out and made for the landing. When I reached there I informed Mr. McCormack that the place was deserted. He with some of the men came up second time, so as to make sure, but unfortunately the first impression was only too true. Mr. McCormack and myself proceeded to the lightroom where everything was in proper order. The lamp was cleaned. The fountain full. Blinds on the windows etc. We left and proceeded on board the steamer. On arrival Captain Harvie ordered me back again to the island accompanied with Mr. McDonald (Buoymaster), A. Campbell and A. Lamont who were to do duty with me till timely aid should arrive. We went ashore and proceeded up to the lightroom and lighted the light in the proper time that night and every night since. The following day we traversed the Island from end to end but still nothing to be seen to convince us how it happened. Nothing appears touched at East landing to show that they were taken from there. Ropes are all in their respective places in the shelter, just as they were left after the relief on the 7th.

"On [the] West side it is somewhat different. We had an old box halfway up the railway for holding West landing mooring ropes and tackle, and it has gone. Some of the ropes it appears, got washed out of it, they lie strewn on the rocks near the crane. The crane itself is safe.

"The iron railings along the passage connecting railway with footpath to landing had started from their foundation and broken in several places, also railing round crane, and handrail for making mooring rope fast for boat, is entirely carried away. Now there is nothing to give us an indication that it was there the poor men lost their lives, only that Mr. Marshall has his seaboots on and oilskins, also Mr. Ducat has his seaboots on. He had no oilskin, only an old waterproof coat, and that is away. Donald McArthur has his wearing coat left behind him which shows, as far as I know, that he went out in shirt sleeves. He never used any other coat on previous occasions, only the one I am referring to."

Moore and a couple of crewmen stayed at the lighthouse to keep it running, and Robert Muirhead, a Northern Lighthouse Board superintendent, was sent for. In his report, he gives more details of the destroyed west landing:

> "Owing to the amount of sea, I could not get down to the landing place, but I got down to the crane platform 70 feet above the sea level. The crane originally erected on this platform was washed away during last winter, and the crane put up this summer was found to be unharmed, the jib lowered and secured to the rock, and the canvas covering the wire rope on the barrel securely lashed round it, and there was no evidence that the men had been doing anything at the crane. The mooring ropes, landing ropes, derrick landing ropes and crane handles, and also a wooden box in which they were kept and which was secured in a crevice in the rocks 70 feet up the tramway from its terminus, and about 40 feet higher than the crane platform, or 110 feet in all above the sea level, had been washed away, and the ropes were strewn in the crevices of the rocks near the crane platform and entangled among the crane legs, but they were all coiled up, no single coil being found unfastened. The iron railings round the crane platform and from the terminus of the tramway to the concrete steps up from the West landing were displaced and twisted. A large block of stone, weighing upwards of 20 cwt, had been dislodged from its position higher up and carried down to and left on the concrete path leading from the terminus of the tramway to the top of the steps.
>
> "A life buoy fastened to the railings along this path, to be used in case of emergency had disappeared, and I thought at first that it had been removed for the purpose of being used but, on examining the ropes by which it was fastened, I found that they had not been touched, and as pieces of canvas was adhering to the ropes, it was evident that the force of the sea pouring through the railings had, even at this great height (110 feet above sea level) torn the life buoy off the ropes."

He concluded, "From evidence which I was able to procure I was satisfied that the men had been on duty up till dinner time on Saturday the 15th of December, that they had gone down to secure a box in which the mooring ropes, landing ropes etc. were kept, and which was secured in a crevice in the rock about 110 ft (34 m) above sea level, and that an extra large sea had rushed up the face of the rock, had gone above them, and coming down with immense force, had swept them completely away."

While this appears to make sense, it would mean these experienced lighthouse keepers had broken a fundamental rule—that one man must stay at his post at all times. Some historians have suggested that McArthur ran to warn his coworkers when he saw rough seas coming for them. The West landing is near a geo, a cave or narrow cleft that lets out onto the sea with a second opening on land. When a high wave passes into the cave's sea entrance, it gets funneled through the cave and comes shooting out the land entrance, like a geyser. Geos are a truly impressive and intimidating sight. McArthur must have rushed outside, knocking over the kitchen chair and leaving behind his waterproof, although inexplicably closing the doors behind him, only to suffer the same fate as the others.

This seems to be the most logical explanation for the men's disappearance, but it does not explain the strange entries found in the lighthouse journal. The one for December 12th was written by Marshall, the second assistant, who described "severe winds the likes of which I have never seen before in twenty years." It mentioned that James Ducat, the Principal Keeper, had been "very quiet," and Third Assistant William McArthur had been crying. Everyone who knew McArthur knew him as a fun-loving brawler, not someone prone to tears.

The entry for the next day said that the storm was as bad as ever and that all three men were praying. The final entry on December 15th said only, "Storm ended, sea calm. God is over all."

This journal brings up several unanswerable questions. First off, there was no storm on December 12th and 13th. The Isle of Lewis, which is well inhabited and only 10 miles away, reported that the weather was fair and there was no localized storm to the west. A storm did blow in on December 17th, but that was two days after the last journal entry.

One might also wonder why the men were so upset. They were experienced islanders, snug in a well-built lighthouse, well above sea level. They had nothing to fear. Did they have a premonition of their own deaths? And what did that final line mean? The answers will probably never be known.

One oft-cited Scottish mystery turns out not to be as mysterious as once thought. Much ink has been spilt over the so-called vitrified ancient forts of Scotland. Of course, Scotland is full of forts of various styles, made over the centuries, but one type of fort truly stands out. These are dry stone walls that ring the tops of hills, measuring up to 12 feet high, and considerably more in thickness. Sometimes there are two or three walls in concentric rings. Strangely, parts of them have been burned with a heat so intense that the stone has vitrified, the individual stones melting together to make a glassy surface. This is generally done on the exterior surface of the wall, but there are some examples of it being done on the inside of the wall. In these cases, the wall was actually hollow, with a fire burning inside to vitrify both sides, and then filled in with rubble once cooled.

More than 60 examples are known in Scotland, and date to the Iron Age (700 BC-500 AD) and the Early Medieval Period (500-900 AD). While a few examples of vitrified forts have been found in Ireland and on the European mainland, the majority are in Scotland.

Just why and how these stones walls were subjected to such intense heat has puzzled generations of archaeologists, and led to more than a few wild theories. Some books even claim they were attacked by UFOs using lasers or nuclear weapons!

In fact, no such wild theories are needed. Close investigation of the forts shows some interesting details. Only parts of each wall are vitrified, and not always evenly so. Also, there is no other significant damage to the walls, so the vitrification doesn't appear to have occurred during an attack.

In 1934 and again in 1937, archaeologists Wallace Thorneycroft and Vere Gordon Childe decided to build a wall of native stone and vitrify it by heaping a large pile of brush and wood against the wall and continually feeding it for a period of time. They managed to vitrify the stone once the fire reached a temperature of 1100° Celsius (2012° Fahrenheit). By way of comparison, a blacksmith's forge must reach 1300° Celsius in order to separate iron from ore, so such a fire was well within the capacity of Iron Age technology. Their wall, which measured six feet high and six feet thick, collapsed after three hours, but the base was left standing, vitrified just like the walls found at the Scottish forts.

Of course, this leaves people wondering why the ancients would do this to their forts. At first, archaeologists thought the process was to strengthen the wall, but experiments show that it in fact weakens it by making the stone brittle, and in any case, it wasn't applied to the entire wall. It also doesn't seem to have been done by attackers, since they would have to pile up a huge load of lumber and constantly feed the fire as spears and arrows rained down upon them. The end result would have been a bunch of dead men and an only slightly weakened wall, or a partial collapse at best, that would have been too hot to charge through.

Other theories involve rituals - the go-to explanation for archaeologists when faced with something incomprehensible. Some researchers hold that it was a form of symbolic destruction, a kind of cleansing before the fort was abandoned. Since no written record survives from that period, this theory cannot be proven, and thus the mystery of the vitrified forts, though stripped of its paranormal glamour, has not been solved.

Though UFOs didn't come out of the sky to vitrify the walls of ancient Scottish forts, strange things do occasionally fall from the skies over Scotland, and they've been falling for a long time. In 1825, a shower of herrings fell near Loch Leven. That's right, herrings—the fish. Fish falls are actually reported all over the world, as are frog falls, and other downpours of unlikely animals and objects.

Three years later, herrings fell again in the Firth of Dingwall. In 1830, they fell on the Isle of Ula. All of these fish came down with the rain in blustery conditions, leading to the theory that a waterspout had lifted them out of a nearby body of water and set them down on land.

The British Isles have reported a number of falls, including those of frogs, bits of metal, and even peanuts. In 1995, Nellie Straw of Sheffield, England was driving through a severe storm in

Scotland when suddenly, hundreds of frogs started coming down with the rain. In the modern world, airplanes can be used as an explanation, assuming fun-loving pilots would be motivated to drop frogs from their planes during a rainstorm, but dealing with reports from the 19th century is a little more difficult. Do frogs get picked up by waterspouts too? Science has no answer. In any case, Scotland seems partial to herrings.

Scotland also seems to be partial to "star jelly," the traditional name given to little white blobs of gelatinous material found in fields at various times of the year in Scotland and Northern England. They evaporate fairly quickly, and have been the subject of scant study in the scientific community, despite the fact that they're a long-running mystery. Folklore explains that these blobs are actually the stuff left over from falling stars.

Star jelly has been falling for so long that it has even made it into Scottish literature. Sir Walter Scott put it in his novel *The Talisman*, in which the character of the hermit says, "Seek a fallen star and thou shalt only light on some foul jelly, which in shooting through the horizon, has assumed for a moment an appearance of splendour."

Star jelly is also called astral jelly by those who lean toward a paranormal explanation. Others call it star rot, star shot, and for those who just think the entire thing is more funny than mysterious - moon poo.

While astronomers dismiss the idea that star jelly comes from shooting stars (which are actually meteors made of rock and/or metal), science has yet to come up with an adequate explanation. A few years ago, the BBC Outdoors program launched an investigation into star jelly and got frustratingly vague responses from various experts. The main theory is that the little white clumps are frog ovaries. They look identical to them, and ovaries are distasteful and somewhat toxic, so perhaps birds and other predators are eating frogs and regurgitating the ovaries. Nature photographer and television presenter Chris Packham gathered a sample of star jelly and sent it to the Natural History Museum in London to be DNA tested. The test came back as frog with small traces of magpie. Packham then concluded that a magpie had eaten a frog and regurgitated the ovaries.

But don't be too quick to consider that as proof and the mystery solved, because a DNA test by the BBC Outdoors program on some star jelly came back inconclusive, and several experts told the show that they believe the strange gunk isn't from an animal at all. There is also the question of why it's found in large clumps in open fields, and not regularly in places where frogs congregate. Also, frogs ovulate in March and April, but star jelly can be found at any time of the year, even in the dead of winter.

Another theory is that star jelly is a type of fungi. Two Scottish scientists interviewed by the program were stumped. Algae expert Hans Sluiman of the Royal Botanic Garden in Edinburgh said it appears to be neither plant nor animal. Fungi expert Andy Taylor at the Macaulay Institute in Aberdeen found filaments of fungus in a sample of star jelly, but concluded that it was growing inside the substance and not actually creating it.

An Ancient Irish Mystery

Ireland is rich in old stories. The most enduring and global is that of St. Brendan, a 6th century monk who traveled around Britain and Ireland, establishing churches in lands that were still largely Pagan. He also visited remote islands to the west of Ireland, places that became areas of refuge for Irish monks seeking to cut themselves off from the world. Some people believe he even visited North America.

The idea comes from a 9th century manuscript, titled *The Voyage of St. Brendan*. It's a fabulous tale of Brendan and his followers boarding a *currach*—a small, round-bottomed boat made of leather stretched around a wooden frame—and sailing off into the Atlantic on a seven year voyage to find the Promised Land.

After 40 days, they came to an island with steep and rocky cliffs, and waterfalls on the cliffs. There, they discovered a palace filled with food. The devil tempted one of St. Brendan's followers to steal a silver bridle from the palace, but the saint managed to cast the devil out and save the man's soul. Their next stop took them to an island that never experienced winter and had sheep as big as oxen.

Then the real fun began. During the next stage of their trip, they were lifted up by a whale, pestered by demons, chatted with a talking bird, were tossed about by a three-month storm, met Judas Iscariot stranded on a tiny rock in the middle of a stormy sea, and had many other fabulous adventures. The saint, of course, got them through it all with the power of prayer.

A medieval depiction of Brendan and the whale

Here's a typical passage:

> "One day a fish of enormous size appeared swimming after the boat, spouting foam from its nostrils, and ploughing through the waves in rapid pursuit to devour them. Then the brethren cried out to the Lord: 'O Lord, who hast made us, deliver us, Thy servants;' and to St. Brendan they cried aloud: 'Help, O father, help us;' and the saint besought the Lord to deliver His servants, that this monster might not devour them, while he also sought to give courage to the brethren in these words: 'Fear not, you of little faith, for God, who is always our protector, will deliver us from the jaws of this monster, and from every other danger.'
>
> "When the monster was drawing near, waves of immense size rushed on before it,

even up to the gunwale of the boat, which caused the brethren to fear more and more; but St. Brendan, with hands upraised to heaven, earnestly prayed: 'Deliver, O Lord, Thy servants, as Thou didst deliver David from the hands of the giant Goliath, and Jonas from the power of the great whale.'

"When these prayers were uttered, a great monster came into view from the west, and rushing against the other, spouting flame from its mouth, at once attacked it. Then St. Brendan spoke: 'Behold, my children, the wonderful work of our Saviour; see here the obedience of the creature to its Creator: await now the end in safety, for this conflict will bring no evil to us, but only greater glory to God.'

"Thereupon the rueful monster that pursued the servants of God is slain, and cut up in their presence into three parts, and its victor returned whence it came. Next day they saw at a distance an island full of herbage and of wide extent. When they drew near it, and were about to land, they found the hinder portion of the monster that was slain. 'Behold,' said St. Brendan, 'what sought to devour you. Do you now make your food of it, and fill yourselves abundantly with its flesh.'"

Once past these dangers, Brendan and his followers passed through sea choked with ice before coming across a spacious land of thick forest, as much of the northeast coast of North America was at that time. Sailing further, they came to some low, sandy islands that could have been the barrier islands along the Middle Atlantic. Details are sketchy, and for centuries historians have puzzled over the vague geographical hints in an attempt to link them with actual places in the North Atlantic. For example, one island was "remarkably flat, almost level with the sea, without a tree or anything that waved in the wind; but it was of wide extent, and covered over with white and purple flowers." This could be many places in the North Atlantic, from the Orkney Islands just north of Scotland to Arctic Canada. Strangely, this island, and most other places they visited, had already been inhabited by monks.

After a journey of seven years, St. Brendan and his monks finally made it to the Promised Land, and he found it to be a vast country thick with trees and fruit where the sun never sets. Some have tried to link this to northern Canada, where there is almost no night in the summertime. They didn't meet any Native Americans, who were living throughout the region at the time, but they did meet a holy man, or angel, who spoke their language and told them their pilgrimage was over and it was time to go home.

This account, and that of the Vinland Saga of the Norsemen, were both widely known during the Renaissance, and Christopher Columbus himself consulted them before making his historic voyage to the New World. Some medieval maps even drew "St. Brendan's Isle" as being far out in the Atlantic.

A posthumous portrait depicting Columbus

While some modern researchers concede there is much fable in the story, they believe Irish monks could have really sailed across the ocean to the New World. To prove the voyage could have been made, sailor and adventurer Tim Severin built a currach out of traditional materials. The boat measured 36 ft. (11 m), had two masts, and was made of 49 ox hides, lashed together with leather thongs. In 1976, he and his crew sailed it 4,500 miles (7,200 km) from Ireland, across the North Atlantic, to Newfoundland. Everyone made it safely.

It was an epic trip, and Severin's book on the adventure became a bestseller, but while Severin's voyage proves that St. Brendan could have made it across the Atlantic, it doesn't mean that he actually did. After all, unlike St. Brendan, Severin had the advantage of knowing exactly where he was going.

There is, however, evidence that Irish monks got at least part way there. The Faroe Islands, about halfway between Scotland and Iceland, were first settled sometime between the 4th and 6th centuries CE, well before Viking colonization in the 9th century. While material evidence is scant, some scholars believe the settlers were Irish or Scottish monks. Also, in 825, an Irish monk named Dicul wrote that his brethren had colonized islands far to the north of Scotland before the Vikings did.

The Faroes were the first stop in Norse expansion across the North Atlantic. From there, they went on to Iceland, Greenland, and eventually to North America, around 1000.

The first stop was Iceland, which was settled by the Norse around the year 874. Many of the earliest texts from Iceland mention Irish and Scottish monks called *papar*, similar to the Latin and Old Irish words for "Pope." There are also the remains of a settlement at Herjólfsdalur, on the Westman Islands, off Iceland's south coast, that was occupied in the 7th century, well before the Norse said they had made it there. The dating of this site, however, is a matter of dispute in archaeological circles.

The Norseman Erik the Red landed on Greenland in 982, and he returned a few years after to explore and set up two colonies. Though they didn't find any people, they did find the remains of settlements, stone tools, and skin boats. The Norse identified these as belonging to the people of North America they later encountered, but could they have been made by Irish monks, instead? They had already made it halfway across the Atlantic to Iceland. If they had made it to Greenland, they might have discovered there was better land a short sail away in North America, as the Norse had.

Illustration of Erik the Red from Arngrímur Jónsson's *Gronlandia*

The evidence for this, however, is lacking. There is no archaeological evidence supporting the presence of Irish colonies in North America. No settlements – such as the famous Skellig Michael (recently featured in *Star Wars: The Force Awakens*) – have survived and no distinctly Irish medieval artifacts have been found. Thus, unless archaeologists dig up any solid proof from the ground, the Legend of St. Brendan will have to stay a legend. Irish-Americans can at least be comforted by the fact that he could have made it, and even if he didn't, his name will always be associated with the exploration of the New World.

Strange Irish Creatures of the Deep

While their Scottish neighbors to the east can boast having the most well-known lake monsters–the most famous, of course, at Loch Ness–the Irish can also claim to have a few beasties living in their lakes as well.

The most famous is Muckie, said to dwell in the Lakes of Killarney, a series of three lovely lakes in County Kerry. In recent years, several people claim to have sighted a large grey object with two or more humps rising above the surface before quickly disappearing into the depths. In 2003, when a team of marine biologists did a sonar scan of the lakes to detect the fish population, they noted a large object in the water that they couldn't identify.

Muckross Lake, one of the Lakes of Killarney

A picture of the lakes from Torc Mountain

Then there are the fearsome Dobhar-chú, said to lurk in many Irish rivers. Unlike the reclusive, benign Muckie, the Dobhar-chú are not to be trifled with. Having haunted Irish rivers since ancient times, they often surface in pairs or groups to drag unlucky people into the water. They are said to look like giant otters or a mix between a dog and a fish. Dobhar-chú means "water hound" in Old Irish. In modern Irish, it means "otter," further obscuring the real nature of this beast.

Whatever they are, they still capture the imagination of the rural Irish, who have no doubt of the creatures' existence. Their fierceness is attested on a 17th century gravestone, called the Kinlough Stone, dedicated to the memory of a woman named Gráinne, who was attacked by the Dobhar-chú as she was washing the family's clothes by the shore of Glenade Lough. Her screams attracted her husband, who killed the beast, but not before his wife had succumbed. As the Dobhar-chú fell, it let out a whistling sound summoning another Dobhar-chú, probably its mate. The farmer managed to kill that one as well.

A Bango Art depiction of a Dobhar-chú

While rare, sightings of the Dobhar-chú still occur today. Irish artist Sean Corcoran and his wife described the creature as covered with gray fur except for its orange webbed feet in 2003.

The seas around the Emerald Isle are thick with monsters. Perhaps the most famous of these has been sighted for many years off the coast of Kilkee, County Clare. Kilkee became a popular beach resort in Victorian times, and visitors who flocked to the little village on Ireland's west coast to stroll along the picturesque shore got to see more than they'd expected.

The Kilkee cliffs

In 1850, numerous witnesses spotted a large sea serpent sunning itself near the shore. It was said to have resembled many other sea monsters spotted in the 19th century—a long, serpentine beast with a large head and smooth gray or black skin. The creature was seen numerous times, making headlines in September of 1871, when several witnesses recounted their sightings for the press. Europe's popular illustrated newspapers, filled with engravings of current events, showed a long, snakelike creature with flippers and huge eyes, threatening a group of ladies on shore with its fanged maw. A gentleman is shown bravely defending the "weaker sex" as they flee in horror, but more it's more than likely the man was running as well.

A report in the October 1871 edition of *Daily Doings* said of the monster, "It had an enormous head, shaped somewhat like a horse, while behind the head and on the neck was a huge mane of seaweed-looking water; the eyes were large and glaring, and, by the appearance of the water behind, a vast body seemed to be beneath the waves."

Sightings of sea serpents were fairly common in the age of steam, but sadly, there are fewer sea monsters to contend with now. Some people will scoff and say that modern people are less likely to believe in such nonsense, while others point out that the pollution of our oceans might have made them go extinct, or at least put them on the endangered list.

They haven't disappeared completely, however. In 2013, some fishermen in Lough Foyle, which opens onto the North Channel, caught a weird sea creature on film. The minute of footage shows a dark gray or black hump moving smoothly through the water. The hump was peaked at the top and had several irregular bumps on its surface. It sped along at about the speed of a man jogging, neither rising nor falling for several seconds before gradually descending into the water and out of sight. It left little wake and seemed to be headed out to sea. The film shows it passing between the photographer's boat and another boat, thus allowing for an estimate of the hump's size. It appears to rise about a meter above the water and to be two or so meters long. Of course, this is only the part that was visible above the water. Its actual dimensions could be much greater.

Irish Ghosts, Banshees, and Phantom Ships

For those who believe in them, an ancient land like Ireland is bound to be thickly populated by ghosts. Irish folklore is rich in ghost stories, and many sightings and strange experiences continue to the present day.

One lovely tradition from the 19th and 20th centuries says that the spirits of migrants who have died overseas would return home as seagulls or sea mist. But not all Irish ghost stories are as poetic; in fact, some are downright ghoulish. For example, the little town of Rathkeale, County Limerick, stands Holy Trinity Church and its historic cemetery. While the present church is relatively recent, having been built in 1831, there has been a church in that location for more than 700 years, and the cemetery has graves dating back more than 300 years. For many years, the graveyard is said to have been haunted by a female specter so frightening to look upon that those who see her have their hearts stop.

One local man, braver than most, stayed in the graveyard overnight armed with his trusty sword, waiting for the ghost. Why he thought he'd be able to kill a ghost with a sword is anyone's guess, but he had great faith in God and the Virgin Mary, and for an Irishman, that was good enough. The ghost duly appeared and the man looked at it full in the face, fearing nothing.

He took one swipe at it with his sword, cut off the ghost's arm, and the phantom woman vanished out of sight. The man spent the rest of the night praying the woman's restless spirit would be laid to rest, and it never appeared again.

Oddly, another supernatural woman made her appearance in a graveyard in the same small town, but this time, the experience was far more benign (as discussed further below in the section on Marian apparitions).

As is the case in other old countries, many historic buildings are said to be haunted. One of these haunted buildings is Ross Castle, on the shores of Lough Sheelin, County Meath, which has earned the dubious distinction of being considered the most haunted castle in Ireland. The region had a bloody history in the Middle Ages, having been just "beyond the pale," meaning it was past the area of English control. With the English to the east and the native Celtic tribes to the west and north, the area became a constant battleground. Several castles and strongholds dotted the landscape at the time. Ross Castle was built in 1533 by the English to control the River Inny where it enters Lough Sheelin. This was the outer limits of their territory, and thus the castle was of crucial strategic importance. It suffered many sieges and battles before it was eventually leveled by Oliver Cromwell after it had been used as a base for Irish rebels.

A 19th century picture of Ross Castle

A modern picture of Ross Castle

Cromwell

Naturally, such a place was ripe for haunting. Most of the stories center around Richard Nugent, the 12th Lord of Delvin, the man who built the castle in 1536. He was a tough and cruel man, even by the standards of those tough and cruel times, and it eventually earned him the nickname of the Black Baron. Some locals say this was due to his having hanged an innocent beggar whom he accused of stealing some bread, even though there had been no evidence against the man.

Blood does not always run true, and the Black Baron's daughter was said to be as kind as he was cruel; as sweet as he was bitter. Her name was Sabina, and everyone loved her. She could often be seen strolling on the shores of the Lough Sheelin, where she would admire the view and speak with anyone she met without prejudice. Even though she was the daughter of an English military occupier, she chatted happily with the Irish peasants she met. This made her as well loved by the Irish as she was by the English.

Given her position, she was supposed to be accompanied by a chaperone at all times. Sabina had a free spirit, however, and often slipped away to walk alone, knowing she had nothing to fear.

It was on one of those solitary walks that she met a handsome young man and started talking with him. His name was Orwin O'Reilly, the son of a local Irish chief. They formed an instant attraction for one another and promised to meet again, soon. Neither Sabina nor Orwin were so young and innocent as to be unaware of the dangers of their friendship. Their fathers were enemies, after all, as were their respective peoples, and they had to have their meetings in the utmost of secrecy. As the meetings continued, their love grew, as did their despair. They wanted to get married, but this was impossible; simply meeting together as they did was bound to cause a war.

Like other star-crossed lovers throughout time, they decided to elope. One night, Sabina slipped out of Ross Castle and crept to the shore of Lough Sheelin, where Orwin waited for her with a boat. They rowed out across the water, their young hearts filled with hope for the future that they would settle down somewhere far away from their warring fathers and start a new life under new names.

As the lovers talked of the future, a sudden storm blew in from the west. Orwin tried to manage the oars while Sabina bailed desperately, but it was no use. The storm grew stronger, eventually overturning the boat and sending the couple into the frigid waters of Lough Sheelin. Sabina was found the next morning, washed up on shore and barely alive. She was carried back to Ross Castle where she lay unconscious for three days. When she, at last, awoke, it was to terrible news - her lover, Orwin, had been found as well, but he had drowned. Sabina fell into despair and locked herself in the tower, refusing to eat or drink until she, too, had died. Perhaps she hoped to join her lover on the other side, but it was not to be. Instead, she haunts the castle, endlessly roaming its halls or looking over its battlements with the hope of finding her long-lost lover, her sorrowful wailing awakening residents.

A picture of Lough Sheelin

The Black Baron is sometimes seen, too. According to local legend, Sabina's stay on this earth will only end when her evil father has atoned for his misdeeds.

Ross Castle is now a bed and breakfast, and online guest reviews tell of the many strange occurrences happening there. Besides seeing both ghosts, one visitor was scratched on the arm by invisible nails, cutting so deeply they drew blood. Others hear strains of old music, feel sudden drops in temperature, and are awoken by phantom footsteps in the hall. The hauntings center around the tower, the oldest part of the castle, although entities have been seen, heard, and felt all over the newer portions built in the last two centuries, as well. Of all the rooms in the bed and breakfast, the most haunted is the Whisper Room, so called because guests there often hear whispering that seems to come from thin air.

Even for those who don't believe in ghosts, a stay in an old castle is a memorable experience. Ross Castle is decorated with suits of armor, stuffed birds, and even a buffalo's head, which–while not exactly Irish–certainly adds an odd atmosphere to the place. Several other Irish castles have been turned into similar B&Bs as well, such as Clontarf Castle in Dublin, Ashford Castle in County Mayo, Ballynahinch Castle in County Connemara, and many more. All of them, it seems, have a ghost story to tell.

Many of Ireland's traditional pubs are believed to be haunted as well. John Kavanagh's in Dublin, locally known as "The Gravediggers Pub," dates back to 1833, making it a relative youngster when compared to the city's historic buildings. It gets its nickname thanks to being located next to the historic Glasnevin Cemetery, where many prominent Irish figures, such as Irish nationalists Stewart Parnell and Roger Casement, are buried. The pub was where the gravediggers were known to refresh themselves after a hard day's work, often making their orders by throwing a clod of dirt against the wall in order to alert the barkeep. At night, it was said to be the den of grave robbers. It is still a solemn place, with no singing or dancing allowed, and no television that ruins the atmosphere of so many old pubs. There isn't even a telephone.

Parnell

Casement

On some quiet nights, a visitor might notice an old man in an out of date tweed suit, sipping a pint at the end of the bar. He doesn't speak, and is so unremarkable that no one bothers to speak to him, but when he finishes his drink he simply fades away.

The most famous Irish ghost is, of course, the banshee, a female spirit that lets out a loud wail at night. There are two traditions that explain their existence. One is that she is the ghost of a woman who lost her children before she died. This tradition can be found in other cultures as well, such as the Mexican belief in *La Llorona* ("The Weeping Woman"). The other explanation for the banshee is that of a fairy, come to mourn humans who have died–often but not necessarily children–or to warn a family that they would soon suffer a loss. The term banshee comes from the Irish *bean sidhe*, meaning "woman of the fairies." The banshee was attached to certain families, always of the aristocratic class, who would hear her mournful keening before one of their number was about to die.

In Shane's Castle on the shores of Lough Neah in Antrim, there's a room reserved for a banshee. She is said to appear regularly, sometimes hooded and hard to see, sometimes looking like a beautiful but mournful young maiden. Family tradition states that the banshee is actually the spirit of a member of the castle's hereditary family, the O'Neills. It was a girl named Kathleen, who was taken away by the fairy folk, only allowed to return when a member of the family was about to die.

Kenneth Allen's picture of the ruins of Shane's Castle

Another female spirit is the fearsome Demon Bride. This baleful ghost has haunted the Errigal-Truagh Graveyard in County Monaghan for more than two centuries. It waits until there is a funeral in the graveyard, watching the mourners carefully. As the grieving family and friends file out of the cemetery, one person will often linger for a moment. If this final mourner is a young man, the Demon Bride appears as a beautiful young woman and chats with the fellow, whose sadness turns to interest at the attentions of the comely stranger. The Demon Bride tells the young man how handsome he is and how much she fancies him. At this point, she gets him to promise to return to the cemetery exactly one month later, in order to get "better acquainted." They seal the promise with a kiss, a kiss so passionate that the man is fired with lust.

At that point the lady vanishes. The young man blinks in surprise, not sure what has happened. As he staggers out of the graveyard, he remembers the local tale of the Demon Bride, and realizes he's lost his soul to a spirit from the other side, which makes him go mad, his raving terror destroying his health until he dies. Exactly one month after he's met the Demon Bride, he keeps his promise by being buried in the Errigal-Truagh Graveyard.

Besides dead individuals stalking the land and Ireland's old buildings, there are also phantom ships that roam the seas in the area. Several of them are known from the vicinity of Wexford, where they seem to gather.

One morning in 1915, a tugboat left Wexford Harbour, heading for the Tuskar Rock lighthouse off Ireland's southeast coast. World War I was in the process of ripping Europe apart, and the crew had been told to keep a sharp eye out for warships and U-boats. As the boat got out into the open ocean, the crew spotted a warship in the distance, headed in their direction. As was normal for the time, the crew raised the Union Jack to identify themselves. Ireland had not yet achieved its independence, and the Union Jack was the flag the Irish crew flew, whether they liked it or not. Hoping the warship wasn't German, they watched with bated breath to see which flag the ship would send up. But the ship didn't put up a flag. It passed close by the tugboat, and while the crew was able to see the men on board, they could not read the name of the ship on the prow, nor could they see any signs to identify the ship's country of origin.

When the tugboat arrived at the Tuskar Rock lighthouse, they told the lighthouse keeper what they had seen, and were shocked to learn that the keeper hadn't seen any warships pass by at all that day. The lighthouse keeper had a splendid view of the entire area and would certainly have spotted any vessel as it passed, especially if it were a warship in a time of national emergency. The warship was never seen again, and no one ever discovered which side it belonged to, or if it even existed at all.

A very different kind of tugboat lurks around the Saltee Islands, two small islands three miles off the coast of County Wexford. Sometimes, an unidentified tugboat is seen steaming around the islands, and once darkness falls, strange lights are seen just offshore. When fishermen see this, they stay at home mending their nets and salting the day's catch, because they know these are signs of a bad storm brewing and that it would be suicide to go out on that night.

Another ghost ship is regularly seen off the shore of the Great Saltee, the bigger of the two islands. Around the turn of the last century, two men went out onto the rough seas with a rowboat to see if they could save the crew of a shipwreck off the island's south coast–they never returned. The rowboat sometimes returns to the dock on moonless nights. Though it's always dark when it appears, the boat can be clearly made out, and you can hear the oars as they are pulled from their oarlocks and stowed away.

Apparitions of the Blessed Virgin Mary

Ireland is a deeply religious country. Most people are Catholic, and the Church is a cornerstone of social life. Because of this, it is not surprising there have been several accounts of religious miracles, especially sightings of the Virgin Mary, many of which have occurred in the modern day and have supposedly been caught on camera.

Perhaps the most famous in modern times is the rocking statue of the Virgin Mary at Ballinspittle grotto, a roadside grotto featuring a life-sized plaster statue of Mary on a low hill. On July 22, 1985, Cathy O'Mahony and her mother, who lived near the grotto, stopped by to visit. The grotto has a few benches where the devout can sit and pray while looking up at the statue. As they sat down to pray, they noticed the statue had begun to rock back and forth. Convinced they had seen a miracle, they brought more people to the grotto the next day, and they, too, saw the statue rock.

The grotto

Soon, the little roadside shrine was besieged with thousands of people from across the country. The sightings made international news. In all, an estimated 100,000 people visited the previously little-known shrine that summer. On August 15, the Feast of Assumption, an estimated 20,000 people flooded the area, during which some people claimed to have seen the statue floating in the air. One man told reporters he had seen the face of Jesus superimposed on the statue.

The Catholic Church remained neutral on the subject. Michael Murphy, the Bishop of Cork and Ross, issued a public statement that the worshippers had fallen prey to an optical illusion. He went on to say that "direct supernatural intervention is a very rare happening in life. So, common sense would demand that we approach the claims made concerning the grotto at Ballinspittle with prudence and caution. Before a definite pronouncement could be made by the Church, all natural explanations would have to be examined and exhausted over a lengthy period of time."

Regardless, the events in the Ballinspittle grotto set off a wave of religious sightings across the country. In some 30 locations, other statues of Mary – or various saints – moved, and religious figures appeared on church walls.

Ballinspittle grotto, however, remained the focus of attention, and not all of it good. A group of Pentecostals showed up one day, screamed about idolatry, and smashed the statue with hammers. It was soon repaired and went back to rocking and attracting pilgrims.

On the 30th anniversary of the start of the sightings, the *Irish Examiner* reported that the roadside grotto remained a pilgrimage site. Cathy O'Mahony still insists that what she saw was real, as do several other locals.

In an even stranger story, the July 8, 2009 issue of *The Telegraph* reported that workers cutting down a tree in the cemetery of Holy Mary Parish Church in Rathkeale, County Limerick noticed the stump was shaped like a hooded figure holding a smaller figure. One of the workmen immediately fell to his knees and crossed himself, sure he was seeing an apparition of the Blessed Virgin Mary. Word spread fast in the small town, which has a population of only 1,500, and before long people flocked to see the stump, coming in from other towns and counties. A candlelight vigil attracted an estimated 700 people. Others were more skeptical, including a local priest who said it was "just a tree." The Catholic Church avoids taking positions in such cases for fear the religion will fall into superstition, but it doesn't stop the vigils or pilgrimages from other parishes. The Church says that people getting together to pray is always a good thing.

If that wasn't strange enough, the Virgin Mary appeared again seven years later, this time on the side of a house about 20 miles down the road in Kilmallock. One night in December 2016, someone noticed something unusual on the side of a house on the Riverview Estate—a glistening, sparkling shape that looked like a hooded figure holding a smaller figure. As was the case with the tree stump, this was taken to be the Blessed Virgin Mary with the Baby Jesus. A crowd soon gathered despite the chill, and photos of the shape went viral on the Internet. The shape disappeared the next day, and while many dismissed it as a shape caused by frost, others insisted their housing estate had been treated to a genuine sighting of the Mother of God.

The Irish are generally divided on these apparitions. Many devout Catholics think people are deluding themselves when they think they see a statue floating in the air or the shape of the Virgin Mary in a tree stump. As Bishop Murphy said, the Church feels such miracles are rare. Even the Bible, which is full of miracles, treats them as something special and unusual. Despite these objections, there are many in Ireland who truly believe in these miracles, as it helps them in their faith and in facing life's many challenges. Psychologists and anthropologists point out that waves of religious miracles tend to occur in difficult years. The 1980s saw bad economic times in Ireland, and the Emerald Isle is currently going through another economic recession and experiencing another wave of miracles. Social scientists say that the sightings are a way for people to deal with their troubles. True believers, on the other hand, point out that God makes Himself known at the very times needed to keep people's faith strong.

Fairy Folk

No discussion of Ireland's paranormal traditions would be complete without talking about the fairy folk, or the "wee folk," as the Irish sometimes call them. The Irish use other names, too: the Good People; the Little People; the Noble People; the People of the Hills; and most eloquently, the People Outside Us. In the Irish language, they were also called the *Sidhe* or the *Feadh-Ree*, the origin of the term "fairy."

Fairies were supposed to be fallen angels from when Lucifer rebelled against God. As God was casting them out, St. Michael interceded, asking the Creator not to cast any more out lest Heaven would be empty. God agreed, declaring the angels should remain where they were at that moment. Some had already fallen to Hell, while others were still in Heaven. Others had fallen from Heaven and made it halfway to Hell, thus residing on Earth, and those ones became the fairies.

In traditional Irish culture, fairies weren't considered remote creatures on the edge of reality. Rather, they lived right alongside human beings, and evidence of their existence could be seen everywhere. Prehistoric burial mounds were thought to be their homes– sometimes called a *lios* ("fairy fort"). Ancient flint arrowheads were said to be made by fairies.

Fairies are not necessarily dangerous - in fact, they can be quite helpful – but they are easily offended and must be handled with care. When building a house, people must take care not to build it on one of the fairies' homes or to block one of the fairies' paths. Since the roads of the wee folk are difficult to spot, it's best to test the site. Before building a house, set sticks down where corners of the foundation are to go, and if the sticks are still in place the next day, then everything will be fine. If, however, the sticks have been moved, it is a sign that the fairy folk don't want any construction at that spot, and it's best to find another location.

At the same time, it's unwise to move the location too far away, because having fairies on the property ensures a good harvest and that the flocks and herds will prosper. Fairies shared in the wealth of the farm, as long as the farmer was smart and offered them some of his bounty. In some locations, a bowl of milk or butter was left out for them, a practice that is seen in many places in Europe, and as far away as Denmark. Cows that have just given birth to a calf were held in special esteem, and the first stream of milk from such a cow was shot onto the ground so the fairies could lap it up.

Sharing with the fairies helped get people on their good side, but it was best to be cautious.

Red ribbons were tied to the cows' tails or necks to protect them, and on St. Brigid's Eve, an important festival, crosses made of straw are hung in the byre. St. Brigid's Feast, which falls on February 1, marks the start of agricultural work and was an important festival, even in pre-Christian times. Many strange customs were associated with the feast. For example, on Ireland's coast, fishermen brought shellfish into their homes and placed them in the four corners, in order to ensure a good catch for the rest of the year.

If a child spilled milk on the ground, the parents would state, "That to the fairies, leave it to them and welcome." The child wouldn't be scolded, lest it appear as if the parents begrudged the fairies their due. Similarly, when throwing dirty water out of the house, people called out, "Mind the water." In doing so, they hoped to avoid splashing fairies who may be lurking nearby. Fairies are an arrogant lot, and to ruin their fine clothing with a splash of water would surely invoke their wrath.

In the days when many a farmer was known to supplement his income with the profits from an illegal whisky still, the first drops of any batch were thrown up toward the roof as an offering to Red Willie, a fairy who looked over whisky production and who probably got his name from the florid features he developed as a result of too much drinking. If Red Willie received his offering, he'd be sure to protect the still from the police and the taxman.

If one angered the wee folk, one might find his cow "elf shot," evidenced by a small cut in the skin and the presence of a flint arrowhead nearby. The cow would languish, stop producing milk, and perhaps even die. With so many farmers living on the edge of poverty, the loss of a single cow could be a disaster, so the cunning folk developed many cures for elf-shot cows, one of which was to place a fairy arrow in some water, boil the water, and get the cow to drink it.

Fairies lived much like humans, with homes, farms, families, and livestock. They even had wars. Sometimes, a farmer would set out across his field in the early morning, and in addition to the usual dew, he would see a strange white liquid spread over the grass. This was said to be fairy blood, spilt during a fierce battle the night before.

Just like humans, fairies liked the good things in life. All of their men were handsome, and all their women beautiful. They drank nectar out of flowers and the table settings for their feasts were made of pure gold. Despite their wealth, the fairies coveted fine cattle and beautiful babies, and weren't above stealing them. This was the origin of the infamous "changeling." Sometimes, a mother would put her lovely newborn to bed, only to wake up the next morning to find a sickly, wizened, squalling brat in the crib the next morning. This changeling was said to be a baby rejected from the fairy world. Assuming it survived childhood, it would end up being an evil adult who would cause trouble throughout the district. Cattle could be switched out with changelings as well.

Unbaptized children were in the most danger of being taken. Of course, any good Catholic parent would try to carry out this ritual as soon as possible, but in the more remote areas of the countryside, there might be a long wait. Thus, to keep the fairies at bay, it was a good idea to sew some salt into the baby's clothing.

Children could even be switched while still in the womb. A sure sign the fairies were attempting to do this was that the pregnant woman would suddenly turn sickly. If this happened, one was to open every press and drawer in the house in order to ease childbirth. Once the child was born, they had to be closed immediately up again to trap the fairies inside so they wouldn't be able to take the baby. The fairies had to be kept there until a red coal was placed under the cradle and a branch tied over it—alder for a boy or mountain ash for a girl. Then, the salt had to be sewn into the child's clothing before the occupants of the house could finally open their drawers again.

Some cunning men and women knew the secret to seeing the usually invisible fairies. They developed an ointment–the recipe for which was a closely guarded secret–that when rubbed into the eyes, allowed the user see the invisible world. One had to take care, however, because as everyone knows, the fairies like their privacy. If they ever noticed a human who was able to see them, they'd pop the person's eyes out.

While much of Irish lore deals with placating the wee folk, there are times when fairies actually help humans. Sometimes, a poor farmer will be behind on his rent or taxes and be harassed by the debt collector. When the debt collector heads for the poor family's farm, ready to turn them out for lack of payment, he might meet a stranger on the road who will tell him he intends to pay the family's debt, giving him the exact sum owed. Once the payment has been marked in the ledger, the debt collector returns home, only to discover the coins have turned into leaves in his pocket.

Though the Irish believed in and respected fairies in the olden days, they never worshipped them. Fairies were inferior creatures, lacking an immortal soul, and the Irish believed they would be wiped out forever come the Day of Judgment. Only human beings had a chance at an eternal life in heaven.

Witches, Cunning Folk, and other Magical People

As is the case in all traditional societies, Ireland had its share of people who didn't quite fit in. Some were considered forces of good, while others committed nothing but evil.

Irish witches often appeared as simple farmers or fishermen who happened to have aknowledge of magic. They often sucked the luck out of neighboring farms in order to prosper while others suffered. May Eve and May Day were dangerous times, when people were said to be at the mercy of these witches, as well as fairy folk. It was said the fairy forts lay open at that time and the fairies moved freely about the land. It was at this time that fairies often moved houses, and it was an unwise traveler who ventured out late at night.

Taking advantage of this magical festival, witches would try to steal luck from their neighbors. One way to do this was to remove several bucketfuls of water from a neighbor's well, splashing toward their own house. Throwing salt and holy water into a well would protect people from this. Another method was to draw a rope along the dew of a neighbor's field on May Morn, whispering, "Come all to me." This would bring all the production of milk and butter to the witch's house.

One trick the witches had was to turn themselves into hares and drink milk from the cows at night. The best way to get rid of these magical hares was to shoot them with a silver bullet made from an old florin coin. The florin, a silver coin with a cross stamped on, proved doubly effective against witches, due to the combination of the silver and the cross.

Witches had various secrets and tools of the trade, but none was more powerful than the Dead Man's Hand. This was exactly as it sounds—the hand of a recently departed man, stolen from the graveyard at the stroke of midnight. It was dried and smoked until it had the consistency of leather. The Dead Man's Hand could then be used to cast spells and enact curses. Some of these hands were passed down through generations of witches and have ended up in modern collections.

On the more benign side of the magical arts, there were cunning folk who could be relied upon to perform cures and cast spells to bring good luck and drive away the bad. Some people received this status due to a family tradition of handing it down from generation to generation. Others got it by being born under special circumstances, such as being the seventh son of the seventh son, or having been born after one's father had died.

One group of cunning folk was known to have healed the sick with various herbal remedies. Modern medical science is only just scratching the surface of this old knowledge and has so far found that many traditional cures have at least a partial basis in reality. Other cures, however, don't help at all. Even though the herbalists had some level of success, they were considered to be the lowest level of cunning folk. Ireland's traditional folk preferred magical cures. In fact, the more outlandish the remedy, the more it was in favor.

Take, for example, the cure for ague. This antiquated term referred to any disease causing fever and shivering. To cure someone suffering from ague, the cunning man or woman would wrap a living spider in a cobweb. This was then put into a lump of butter and eaten while the patient was in the midst of a shivering fit.

This disgusting concoction pales in comparison to the cure for epilepsy, which involved taking nine pieces of a dead man's skull, grinding them into powder, and mixing it with a fern called wall rue. The epileptic is supposed to take a spoonful of the stuff on an empty stomach every morning for nine days until he is cured (or begins to hide his ailment in order to avoid taking any more of the medicine). He'd better finish it all, however, because if any was left over, the dead man was bound to return, looking for the missing bits of his skull.

Those suffering from persistent headaches could avoid these horrible cures by going to the most specialized of healers: the measuring doctor. The measuring doctor only worked on certain days, according to some complex numerological formula. If the patient visited on the right day, the measuring doctor would sit the sufferer down and measure the man's head. Measurements were taken from ear to ear across the forehead, from ear to ear over the crown of the head, and diagonally across the head. The diagnosis would always be the same: the patient's head was "too open." To cure this, the measuring doctor would press on the head while whispering certain prayers. The patient would have to return for three days in a row, and each time the measuring doctor would measure and press, measure and press, until finally declaring that the patient's skull had finally closed. Proof of his efficacy was that the measurements he took became smaller each day, until the final diagnosis of a closed skull had taken all of the sufferer's pain away.

For those who didn't trust the cunning folk or who weren't fortunate enough to have one living nearby, there were various cures one could try on oneself. For example, if you suffered from bad vision or sore eyes, a visit to a holy well would help. There were holy wells all over Ireland, many of them attached to old ruins, some of them with Pagan origins. Some of the more powerful holy wells were said to have been able to cure blindness.

Holy wells had to be treated with the proper rituals and reverence. They must be approached with a respectful demeanor, and circumambulated three or nine times, depending on the well. Some wells required you to walk around them, while others required you to go on your hands and knees, but in all cases, it was from east to west, following the path of the sun, a hint at the Pagan origins of the wells. While doing this, the pilgrim must recite Pater Nosters and Ave Marias. After each circuit, the faithful must add a stone to a pile nearby, to be counted by the angels at the time of the Last Judgment. Those with the most stones will go on to the highest level of Heaven. Once this ritual has been completed, the person may approach the well itself, which was usually down a flight of narrow steps to an underground pool. They had to then bathe their face and hands in the well to get the effect of that particular well, or drink the water, if that was what was required. Some wells were known to have cured a whole range of diseases, while others treated eye trouble, arthritis, or other common ailments.

Many wells date to Pagan times, and have standing stones nearby or are shaded by an ash tree, which was a tree sacred to Celtic druids. With these wells, it is customary to give some offering to the tree or stones, usually in the form of a colorful ribbon tied around them. While in ancient times these were offerings to the local spirit, god, or goddess, in Christian times they were, and are, offerings to the patron saint of the well. These offerings should not be removed or the magic will be lost, thus they remain throughout the year, fading and tattering in the wind until nature makes them fall off by themselves.

Holy wells weren't the only places to go to look for a cure. Those with a toothache need only go to a graveyard, kneel down at a grave, say three Pater Nosters, three Ave Marias, and then grab a handful of grass growing on top of the grave. This was to be chewed without swallowed, and bits of it pulled from the mouth and tossed away until it was all gone. It was said that the brave soul who did this would never suffer from a toothache again for as long as he lived.

Some illnesses were caused by the fairies and couldn't be cured by simple remedies. These were called "fairy strokes" and were considered very serious. In these cases, a very effective cure dating far back into Ireland's past was in order. Three rows of salt of equal length had to be placed on a table. The afflicted would then have their arm put around the rows enclosing them, have their head bent over the salt, and the Lord's Prayer would be said three times over each row. Next, take the hand of the patient, who is usually too far gone to perform the spell themselves, and recite, "By the power of the Father, and of the Son, and of the Holy Spirit, let this disease depart, and the spell of the evil spirits be broken! I adjure, I command you, to leave this man/woman (insert name here). In the name of God I pray; in the name of Christ I adjure; in the name of the Spirit of God I command and compel you to go back and leave this man free! AMEN! AMEN! AMEN!"

If the victim of the fairy stroke was a child, there was a different cure. First, all the windows and doors of the house had to be securely shut in order to keep the fairies from seeing what was going on, or they might come in and disrupt the cure. A big fire had to be built, into which a packet of herbs, prepared by one of the cunning folk, was thrown. The child had to be carried around the fire three times, while reciting certain secret phrases provided by the cunning folk and sprinkling holy water into the flame. If the child sneezed three times - a likely occurrence given that the house would be filled with smoke by then – he or she was cured and the curse of the fairies was lifted, never to be put on again. To be on the safe side, however, it was best to tie a small bag around the child's neck containing three red ribbons, the nail from the shoe of an ass, and some hair from a black cat. This needed to be worn for a year and a day.

Similar to the cunning folk were certain priests who were considered to have magical powers to heal and protect. Oddly enough, young priests who had just taken the cloth were considered to be more magical than their older superiors. Also, "silenced priests," those who had been suspended for some infraction, were considered the most powerful of all. Why this is the case isn't quite clear. Perhaps it was the common thread of rebellion found in many Catholic countries, where the Church was revered and mistrusted in equal measure.

These magical priests were relied upon to heal the sick, stop the plans of evil landlords, and bring good luck. Sometimes, they didn't even need to be asked to perform these services. If you could get an article of their clothing or even some dirt from their graves, it might be enough.

Watching the Skies

While Ireland isn't famous for its UFOs - that distinction goes to the United States - the Irish have been seeing them in their skies long before it was trendy to do so.

A global wave of UFO sightings occurred in 1947 after businessman Kenneth Arnold flew a private plane over Mt. Rainier in Washington and reported seeing nine "peculiar looking aircraft" flying in a V formation. He said they were shaped like discs and "flew like a saucer would if you skipped it across the water." The story made international headlines, and the term "flying saucer" was born.

While the wave of UFO sightings in the late '40s and early '50s is often remembered as the first wave of UFO sightings, it was actually the second. The first started a half century earlier in 1896, when mysterious airships were spotted all across North America. While crude airships or dirigibles already existed at the time, the airships people reported seeing were much larger and faster, and they appeared in great numbers across Canada and the United States for a span of 20 years.

They came over to Ireland, too, although they took their time. The first airship sighting occurred in 1909, when, on May 19 of that year, an oblong shape was spotted by residents of Belfast flying over the sea, lit up with a string of brilliant lights.

There was another sighting the next day. On May 21, the *Irish Times* reported that the evening before, a mysterious airship had been seen over Donnybrook by numerous witnesses. One described it as a "large oblong shell," while others said it was shaped like a sphere. It moved over the town at a high altitude at considerable speed, even though the night was still, leading people to conclude it must have been powered instead of being a simple balloon. Earlier that afternoon, a similar airship "illuminated by two strong lights" had been seen on the outskirts of Kingstown (now known as Dún Laoghaire), a few miles to the southeast. The airship was seen to have moved to the southwest, and the Donnybrook sightings told of the craft coming from the west and passing over the town in an easterly direction. Could this have been the same airship having made a loop inland before scaring the good residents of Donnybrook?

It wouldn't be the last time. The next year, some fishermen just off the coast of Doagh, County Donegal got a bad fright. On the evening of May 6, a group of fishermen looked up from their work to watch what they had first thought to be a large steamer on the horizon. It soon became apparent that this was no steamer when the bluish-gray object headed right for the shore a quarter of a mile from them. Thinking it was about to smash on the rocks, they sailed over to it in order to help any survivors.

When they got there, they saw the ship was hovering over the beach, "with a dipping motion, at an average of about 20 feet above sea level." The fishermen described it as "being in the form of a torpedo boat, but larger and broader, and carrying with it a steam-like vapor which prevented detection of its exact shape." Torpedo boats were light, narrow ships built for speed, and as the flying torpedo boat - or whatever it was - passed over the beach, there was a large explosion. Later, when three beached fishing boats were found to have been damaged, the fishermen blamed the mystery airship. It continued inland, passing over a field where it set off another explosion. Steam rose from the field below, and a cow was badly cut up.

At this point, it appeared as if the strange apparition was bombing Ireland. The ship then passed over the town of Legacurry, some twenty miles to the south, and "the residents of the village, hearing deafening noise overhead, rushed out of their houses in a state of consternation. It is stated that the noise did not resemble thunder so nearly as it did the roar of a huge waterfall." Then came "a dull thud, as if of a falling substance." Residents later discovered that a mud bank near the town "had been furrowed as if with a gigantic plough for over twenty yards." It continued to the town of Malin, where it made "a tremendous sound like that of a violent hail storm" before passing out of sight.

The coastguard opined that it could have been one of several dirigibles recently lost at sea, although why a distressed crew would bomb people on the ground rather than signal for help could not be explained. The locals weren't having any of that story, either, and according to the May 14, 1910 edition of the *Dundalk Examiner*, they "[spoke] of the visitation as being of quite an unearthly description, and pray[ed] they may be spared a recurrence of it."

So what were these strange airships? They appeared to be faster and more numerous than the airships that actually existed in their day and their actions were strange. Some UFO researchers theorized that UFO sightings have changed through the years in keeping with the culture of the time. People see a strange object in the sky and try to rationalize it based on what they know. Thus, ancient people saw flying gods or angels, and people in the 19th century and early 20th century saw airships. By the time Kenneth Arnold had made his famous sighting, science fiction was all the rage, so people were prepared to see such strange spaceships. Whether UFOs are, in fact, visitors from outer space remains hotly debated in UFO circles. While it is the majority opinion among Ufologists, others believe the craft to be visitors from another time or dimension, or may even be living creatures.

There have been a host of UFO sightings in modern Ireland. Two spectacular cases will suffice to stand in for the rest. In June 1997, an Aer Lingus flight was heading from Dublin to London when the pilot and copilot noticed a glowing red object with blue and white stripes heading straight for them. They were so startled that they took evasive action. The UFO soon disappeared, and when the pilots reported the incident, air traffic control found no radar record showing another airplane near them at the time.

In another case on May 1, 2011, four witnesses in Arklow, County Wicklow, saw a brilliant white light over the River Avoca. The object appeared to be round in shape and shimmered, changing to other colors. It appeared to be 1,000-2,000 feet above the ground and moved at incredible speed and occasionally stopping abruptly, something that aircraft and meteors cannot do. The witnesses watched it for a little less than a minute before it vanished. One witness told the press that he was a plane spotter and amateur astronomer and had never seen anything like it before.

The Weird and Unexplainable

Perhaps Ireland's strangest mystery is the Jumping Church of Kildemock, located a couple of miles south of Ardee in County Louth. The church is a picturesque old ruin. Its history is unclear, but an archaeological excavation in 1953 uncovered a silver penny from the reign of Edward III who ruled from 1327-1377, so the building must be quite old. It is said to have already been a ruin in the 18th century when it made its claim to fame.

Why this church stands out is immediately apparent to any visitor. The western wall stands three feet off of its foundation. It hasn't fallen; it has simply moved. The foundation is clearly visible and it's quite obvious that the wall, which leans a bit precariously but remains upright, does not stand on any hidden foundation.

How could this happen? There are two stories to explain it, the first being that on Candlemas Day in 1715, a severe storm battered the ruined and abandoned church, blowing the wall off its foundation and settling it safely and intact nearly a meter from its original location. While this explanation stretches credulity, the other tale of how the wall moved is no more likely, unless one believes in miracles. The tale goes that a man who had been excommunicated was buried within the church grounds. The church was so disgusted by this sacrilege that it jumped back, leaving the sinner's grave outside of the church grounds.

The Jumping Church has some fierce competition as Ireland's strangest mystery. Another claimant is a spectacular vision in the sky that occurred on the clear, crisp morning of December 14, 1850. Around 6:30 in the morning, well before dawn, a family in the parish of Dunboe, County Derry saw the eastern horizon grow bright, as if the sun had planned to rise early, but the sun did not rise. Instead, two brightly glowing warships sailed into view in the sky. They stayed in sight for a few minutes before sailing away, only to be replaced by two phantom armies. As the December 31, 1850 edition of the *Northern Whig* reported, "[T]he eastern hemisphere became occupied by a grand panoramic representation of two armies approaching in warlike conflict…so distinctly visible was the representation, that their actual manoeuvres could be distinguished."

The startled family was spared a ghostly battle, because an officer from each army strode forward and fought a duel. The paper further reported that the entire display lasted an hour and a half before fading away to be replaced by the natural dawn.

Such visions were not unknown in the pre-modern era. The night before the Battle of Milvian Bridge in 312 CE, the Roman Emperor Constantine, then a Pagan, saw a vision of a cross in the sky with the words "Conquer by this sign" inscribed upon it. He ordered his soldiers to paint the sign on their shields, and they won the battle the next day, defeating Maxentius, Constantine's rival for the throne. Constantine became the undisputed emperor of the Roman Empire and later made Christianity its official religion. Other similar scenes, especially battles, have often been reported throughout time.

The sighting in Dunboe was not the first such vision in Ireland, nor was it the last. In October of 1796, the residents of the town of Youghal, County Cork saw a vision of a walled town hovering in the sky. The ghostly town reappeared on March 9, 1797, and again in June 1801. This third vision was the clearest, and witnesses described having seen mansions surrounded by bushes and white palings, with a forest growing behind them.

The September 8, 1860 edition of the *Coleraine Chronicle* reported on two such incidents. One which was said to have happened sometime in 1848 was reported by some fishermen on Loch Foyle. While fishing at night, they saw a massive parade of soldiers marching across the sky for some two hours. On September 2, 1860, a line of ships sailing from the eastern edge of the sky to the western appeared to a family in County Donegal. The ships were clearly seen "sailing down a river, whose high banks could be made out behind the ships." Other ships were moored by a fortress on a rock. During the 30 minutes the fleet remained visible, the vision was so clear that the family was able to see sailors as they worked on the deck.

On August 2, 1908, the people of Ballyconneely, Connemara saw a phantom city in the sky for three hours, with an assortment of houses clearly visible.

How might one explain these strange visions? The first reaction would be to dismiss them as a combination of Northern Lights and an overactive imagination. In each case, the sky was clear, so such a natural display would be visible. In the case of the fleet flying over County Donegal, the newspaper reported the vision had disappeared when the sky became cloudy. Note, however, that in each case, the scenes were witnessed by a group of people. Would everyone be able to identify the same objects in a display of the Northern Lights? Displays of the Northern Lights are not uncommon in Ireland, so it would have been quite familiar to people living in a time before electric lighting obscured their view of the night sky in a phenomenon disgruntled astronomers call "light pollution." Another explanation is that they had witnessed a strange fluke of optics that had somehow bent the light from a real scene somewhere else and thrown it as if projected onto the night sky, but how this might have happened is unclear. What does seem clear is that these nocturnal visions have become a thing of the past. No one sees phantom cities and armies in the skies anymore, which in some ways is quite a shame.

A more enduring and no less mysterious occurrence is the sighting of the "Lights of Crusheen," a pair of lights that look like flickering candles and are said to be a portent of doom.

These lights are seen on an island called Inchicronan, along a lake near the little village of Crusheen, County Clare. The island is uninhabited and has been so for many years. It's an interesting place, with a ruined medieval abbey and an old graveyard that has been the final resting place of the people of Crusheen for generations beyond counting. When the lights are seen on the island, the people of Crusheen believe one of their number will soon take up residence in the graveyard.

The lights have been seen ever since the Middle Ages, when, on a cold winter's night, a man from the village braved a storm to cross the causeway leading from the lakeshore to the island. The causeway could be slippery and dangerous in bad weather, and the fact that the man got across at all was a minor miracle. He had a good reason to risk himself; his mother was dying and he wanted to summon a monk to perform Last Rites. The monks were usually happy to help, but the only monk awake that night looked out the window at the foul weather and shook his head. "I'll go tomorrow when the weather has cleared," he said. "She'll keep until then."

Sadly, the woman died that night without the benefit of Last Rites. The monk lived many more years and remained unrepentant. Once he had died, however, God's punishment was swift. From then on, he was doomed to cross that lake to the village any time a spirit had to be taken up to heaven, a place he would never be allowed to enter.

Locals always know when the dead monk has to perform his duty, as two lights appear in the graveyard—one smaller and one larger—bobbing about six feet off the ground as if being carried by invisible people. They slowly cross the lake and enter the village to go to the house where the person is dying.

While this might seem like nothing more than a quaint local superstition, the phenomenon has been photographed numerous times and persists into the modern day. In 1967, physicist Dr. Wilfred Forbes studied the lights and interviewed eyewitnesses, but he was left baffled and unable to explain their origin.

Then there are Ireland's famous and mysterious weasel funerals. To be precise, the creatures called weasels in Ireland are actually Irish stoats (*Mustela erminea hibernica*). For some reason, the folks in rural areas call them weasels. A typical example of a weasel funeral was reported in the September 10, 1954 edition of *The Tyrone Constitution*: "A passing lorry killed a weasel near the residence of Mr. Hughie McGready, Mount Charles, Co Donegal. Messrs Gary Burke, Eugene Burke and Eamon Kelly were working nearby. They noticed the dead weasel on the road, but in ten minutes over fifty weasels had gathered to remove the remains. One weasel dragged the dead one away and was followed by some fifty 'mourners' each marching two abreast."

A picture of a stoat

The idea that weasels have funerals is widespread in Ireland, and it has been reported in Scotland as well. A request by the *Irish Times* for more information of this phenomenon from its readership brought in a flood of mail, some of it reporting on weasel funerals, and others warning that it was dangerous to be around the critters when they honored their dead because they might think the onlookers were the murderers. Actually killing a weasel could get people into some serious trouble, according to a letter sent in by a Mrs. Clark of Ballina, County Mayo: "Some men were cutting a meadow one day when they found some young stoats and killed them. Some time later, one of the men observed an old stoat come up and spit into a can of buttermilk the men had for drinking. The man at once threw away all the buttermilk. He said that had he not seen the stoat spitting into it, and had they drank the milk, they all would have been poisoned." Perhaps the stoat was angry at being called by its actual species.

Either way, it seems that visitors to Ireland should be sure to take weasels and fairies seriously, lest they find themselves in some serious trouble.

Online Resources

Other mysterious titles by Charles River Editors

Other folk history titles by Charles River Editors

Other titles about Britain on Amazon

Other titles about Ireland on Amazon

Further Reading

Cassidy, Eddie. "Crowds still flock to 'moving statue' site at Ballinspittle, three decades on." *Irish Examiner*, July 22, 2015. http://www.irishexaminer.com/viewpoints/analysis/crowds-still-flock-to-moving-statue-site-at-ballinspittle-three-decades-on-343777.html Retrieved January 4, 2017.

Charles River Editors, and Sean McLachlan. *The Vikings in North America: The History and Legacy of the Norse Settlements in Greenland and Vinland.* 2015.

Coleman, Loren and Jerome Clark. *Cryptozoology A to Z: The Encyclopedia of Loch Monsters, Sasquatch, Chupacabras, and Other Authentic Mysteries of Nature.* New York City, NY: Fireside Books, 1999.

Corliss, William R. *The Unexplained: A Sourcebook of Strange Phenomena.* New York City, NY: Bantam Books Inc., 1976.

Cornell, James. *The Monster of Loch Ness.* New York City, NY: Scholastic Book Services, 1977.

Devereux, Paul & Thomson, Ian. *The Ley Hunter's Companion.* London: Thames & Hudson, 1979.

Fort, Charles. *The Complete Books of Charles Fort: The Book of the Damned / Lo! / Wild Talents / New Lands.* London: Dover Publications, Ltd, 1974.

Maple, Eric. *Supernatural England.* London: Robert Hale Ltd, 1977.

Marsden, Simon. *This Spectred Isle: A Journey through Haunted England.* New York City: Barnes & Noble, 2006.

Marwick, Ernest W. *The Folklore of Orkney and Shetland.* London, UK: BT Batsford Ltd., 1986.

McCloskey, Keith. *The Lighthouse: The Mystery of the Eilean Mor Lighthouse Keepers.* Stroud, Gloucestershire, UK: The History Press, 2014.

McGowan, Joe. *Echoes of a Savage Land.* Cork: Mercier Press, 2001.

Michell, John. *The New View over Atlantis.* London: Thames & Hudson, 2001.

Moran, P.F., Archbishop. *The Voyage of St. Brendan the Abbot.* Privately published: Denis O'Donoghue, 1893.

Neil, Arnold. *Shadows in the Sky: The Haunted Airways of Britain.* Stroud, United Kingdom: The History Press, 2012.

Ó Súilleabháin, Seán. *Irish Folk Custom and Belief.* Cork: Mercier Press, 1977.

Pattison, Brynmor. "Holy stir as 'image of Virgin Mary' appears on house in Limerick." *Irish Mirror*, December 2, 2016. http://www.irishmirror.ie/news/irish-news/holy-stir-image-virgin-mary-9381161 Retrieved January 4, 2017.

Roche, Richard. *Tales of the Wexford Coast.* Enniscorthy: Duffry Press, 1993.

Seafield, Lily. *Scottish Ghosts.* David Dale House, Scotland: Waverley Books Ltd, 2009.

Severin, Tim. *The Brendan Voyage: Sailing to America in a Leather Boat to Prove the Legend of the Irish Sailor Saints.* New York City: Modern Library, 2000.

The Telegraph. "Virgin Mary spotted in Irish Tree". July 9, 2009. http://www.telegraph.co.uk/news/newstopics/howaboutthat/5790527/Virgin-Mary-spotted-in-Irish-tree.html Retrieved January 4, 2017.

Underwood, Peter. *Where the Ghosts Walk: The Gazetteer of Haunted Britain.* London, UK: Souvenir Press, 2013.

Watkins, Alfred. *The Old Straight Track: Its Mounds, Beacons, Moats, Sites and Mark Stones.* London: Head of Zeus Ltd, 2015.

Westwood, Jennifer and Jacqueline Simpson. *The Lore of the Land: A Guide to England's Legends, from Spring-Heeled Jack to the Witches of Warboys.* London: Penguin Publishing Company, 2005.

Wilde, Lady. *Irish Cures, Mystic Charms & Superstitions.* New York City: Sterling Publishing Company, Inc., 1991.

Wilson, David. "Crop Circles and the Archaeologist" in *Archaeology Ireland*, Vol. 6, No. 3 (Autumn, 1992).

Free Books by Charles River Editors

We have brand new titles available for free most days of the week. To see which of our titles are currently free, click on this link.

Discounted Books by Charles River Editors

We have titles at a discount price of just 99 cents everyday. To see which of our titles are currently 99 cents, click on this link.

Printed in Great Britain
by Amazon